READING
COMPREHENSION

Nonfiction 1

SADDLEBACK
EDUCATIONAL PUBLISHING

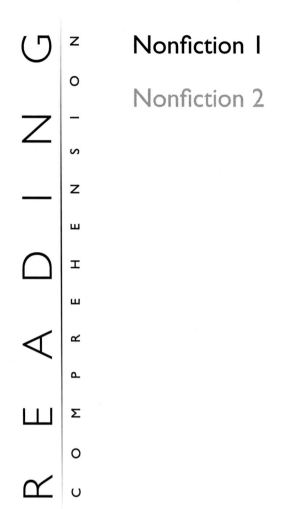

READING COMPREHENSION

Nonfiction 1

Nonfiction 2

SADDLEBACK
EDUCATIONAL PUBLISHING
www.sdlback.com

ISBN-13: 978-1-62250-030-7
ISBN-10: 1-62250-030-X
eBook: 978-1-61247-673-5

Printed in the U.S.A.

20 19 18 17 16   4 5 6 7 8

CONTENTS

The Amazing Charlie Parkhurst

Charlie Parkhurst was a stagecoach driver during the Gold Rush days in California. Nearly every day for 20 years, Charlie took passengers and gold shipments along dangerous roads. Head-on collisions with other stagecoach teams were not unknown on these narrow, dirt pathways. Drivers faced hazards at every turn. Sometimes wild pigs darted out of the woods and spooked the horses!

Charlie was a "regular guy." He smoked cigars, chewed tobacco, played cards, and drank whiskey. His voice was raspy, and his clothing was as dirty as his body. He had lost an eye while trying to shoe a horse, and there was a nasty scar on his face. Once he shot and killed two highwaymen who were trying to rob his stagecoach.

After years of hard work, Charlie retired. By then he was suffering the ravages of rheumatism. This was a

common problem among drivers exposed to years of bad weather. He moved to Santa Cruz, California, and went into the cattle business. Some years later, neighbors remarked that they hadn't seen old Charlie for a few days. On December 31, 1879, they went into his house and found that he had died.

A great surprise awaited them when they dressed the body for burial. They couldn't believe it! Charlie Parkhurst—the rough and tough veteran of the Gold Rush—was in fact a woman.

COMPREHENSION: Circle a letter.

1. The article tells the story of a real person who lived in
   a. colonial days.
   b. the 18th century.
   c. the old West.

2. After retiring, Charlie Parkhurst
   a. left California.
   b. raised livestock.
   c. drove a stagecoach.

3. Charlie could be described as
   a. small and timid.
   b. a troublemaker.
   c. strong and hardworking.

4. The Gold Rush could be described as
   a. polite and orderly.
   b. lively and exciting.
   c. boring and tedious.

The Amazing Charlie Parkhurst   (page 2)

WHY OR WHY NOT?

1. Do you think Charlie's life would have been so adventurous if he'd lived as a woman? Explain your thinking.

    _____

    _____

    _____

    _____

    _____

2. Do you think Charlie Parkhurst was a good-looking person? Explain your reasoning.

    _____

    _____

    _____

    _____

    _____

SYNONYMS: Draw a line to make each match.

1. **ravages**   a. relocated

2. **moved**   b. dangers

3. **cattle**   c. frightened

4. **hazards**   d. harsh

5. **raspy**   e. destruction

6. **spooked**   f. livestock

ANTONYMS: Circle a word.

1. The opposite of *woman* is (*men* / *man*).

2. An antonym of *wild* is (*tame* / *uncivilized*).

3. An antonym of *disrobed* is (*wrapped* / *dressed*).

4. An antonym of *regular* is (*ordinary* / *unusual*).

5. An antonym of *suffering* is (*enjoying* / *enduring*).

6. An antonym of *nasty* is (*attractive* / *repulsive*).

DRAWING CONCLUSIONS

1. Records show that Charlie Parkhurst was born in 1812. How old was he when he died? _____

2. When stagecoach teams collided, who butted heads?

    _____

PICK A PROJECT: Work on the back of this sheet.

● Tell about a modern job that might offer plenty of adventure.

● Look up the *California Gold Rush* in an encyclopedia. Then write three facts about this exciting time.

Are You Afraid of Dogs?

Most dogs are not vicious. In fact, an old saying claims that "a dog is man's best friend." But remember that dogs are *animals*. So it's always wise to be cautious. Even a well-trained dog can be dangerous if it is provoked or frightened.

Common sense can usually help you avoid trouble with strange dogs. Here are some tips from the Humane Society:

- ***Think before you act.*** Don't disturb a dog while it is sleeping, eating, chewing on a toy, or caring for puppies. Never approach a strange dog—especially one that is confined in a car or behind a fence.

- ***Put yourself in the dog's place.*** A dog who doesn't know you may see you as an intruder or as a threat. As far as the dog knows, *you* may be the dangerous one! So try to see a situation as a dog might see it. And remember that it's in a dog's nature to defend its master and home—as well as itself.

- ***In case you are attacked:*** Never turn your back on a dog and try to run away. A dog's natural instinct is to chase and catch you. Never scream and run. Remain motionless, hands at your sides, and avoid eye contact with the dog. Once the dog loses interest in you, slowly back away until it is out of sight.

What should you do if a dog attacks and you fall or are knocked to the ground? Curl into a ball. Put your hands over your ears and remain motionless.

COMPREHENSION: Circle a letter.

1. The article gives you tips on how to
   a. train a dog properly.
   b. behave with strange dogs.
   c. make friends with any dog.

2. Don't approach a strange dog when it's
   a. busy doing something.
   b. playing with its owner.
   c. in need of a bath.

Are You Afraid of Dogs?   (page 2)

3. Looking an angry dog in the eye is

    a. a good way to control it.

    b. seen by the dog as a challenge.

    c. the author's recommendation.

4. The advice in this article comes from

    a. famous dog trainers.

    b. the Humane Society.

    c. the American Kennel Club.

AUTHOR'S PURPOSE

Did the author write this article to *persuade*, to *inform*, or to *inspire*? Explain your thinking.

_____

_____

_____

NOTING DETAILS

What two behaviors mentioned in the article come *naturally* to a dog?

1. _____

    _____

2. _____

    _____

FIGURATIVE LANGUAGE: Circle a letter.

To "put yourself in the dog's place" means

a. to sit where the dog is sitting.

b. to try living outdoors.

c. to think about yourself from the dog's point of view.

VOCABULARY: Circle a letter.

1. To be *confined* is to be

    a. restricted or closed in.

    b. cautioned or warned.

    c. wild and untrained.

2. A *natural instinct* is

    a. learned.

    b. inborn.

    c. reversible.

3. An *intruder* is the opposite of

    a. a harmless cat.

    b. a snarling animal.

    c. an invited guest.

4. A dog that has been *provoked* is

    a. timid and fearful.

    b. annoyed and angry.

    c. calm and relaxed.

5. The opposite of being *humane* is being

    a. kind and compassionate.

    b. cruel and brutal.

    c. intelligent and clever.

PICK A PROJECT: Work on the back of this sheet.

- Tell about a time you had to deal with a dangerous dog.

- Give one more helpful tip about avoiding trouble with strange dogs.

- Explain why you agree or disagree that "a dog is man's best friend."

Have You Ever Had Hic-Hiccups?

Have you ever had a bad case of the hiccups? These sudden halts in breathing accompanied by short gulping sounds can be quite uncomfortable. Charles Osborne of Anthon, Iowa had the longest hiccupping fit ever recorded. He started hiccupping in 1922, while he was weighing a hog before slaughtering it. His hiccups went on until February of 1990! The attack ended as mysteriously as it began. Mr. Osborne led a normal life in spite of his hiccups. He married twice and fathered eight children. He did complain, however, that he had trouble keeping his false teeth in place.

No one knows exactly what gets hiccups started. But we do know that hiccups occur when a large muscle in the chest contracts in jerks. This muscle, called the diaphragm, usually moves up and down in rhythm with a person's breathing. To stop an attack of hiccups, something must happen to shock the diaphragm out of its contractions.

There are lots of so-called "cures" for hiccups. And every single one of them works—sometimes. The next time you start hiccupping, try one of these diaphragm-shockers:

- eating a spoonful of crushed ice
- swallowing a large spoonful of dried breadcrumbs
- sucking on a lemon
- standing on your head and breathing through your nose
- holding your breath

- pressing gently on your closed eyes
- gulping down a tablespoon of peanut butter
- eating a spoonful of sugar
- drinking a big glass of water in one gulp
- an extreme fright

COMPREHENSION: Write **T** for *true* or **F** for *false*.

1. _____ The longest recorded hiccupping fit lasted 68 years.

2. _____ Sweet foods often cause hiccups.

3. _____ There are no known cures for hiccup attacks.

4. _____ When your diaphragm jerks, your breathing jerks, too.

Have You Ever Had Hic-Hiccups?   (page 2)

VOCABULARY: Complete the sentences with words from the article.

1. A person who is inhaling and exhaling is _____.

2. _____ is killing an animal for food.

3. A regular pattern of movement is called _____.

4. The word *wed* is a synonym of _____.

5. The word *stoppages* is a synonym of _____.

6. The word *abnormal* is an antonym of _____.

7. The word *expands* is an antonym of _____.

FACT OR OPINION? Write **F** for *fact* or **O** for *opinion.*

1. _____ Holding your breath is the best-known cure for hiccups.

2. _____ One day a foolproof cure for hiccups will be discovered.

3. _____ Charles Osborne lived in the Midwest.

4. _____ Constant hiccups could make it difficult to eat.

NOTING DETAILS

1. What details in the article support the author's statement that Charles Osborne led a normal life?

_____

_____

2. What detail in the article suggests what Mr. Osborne did for a living?

_____

_____

_____

WORD ANALYSIS

Think about the word *spoonful*. When added to the end of a word, the suffix *-ful* means _____.

Write three more words that end in *-ful*.

_____

_____

_____

PICK A PROJECT: Work on the back of this sheet.

- Tell about a time you had hiccups. Explain how long the attack lasted, and what you did to stop it.

- Describe a "hiccup cure" that is *not* mentioned in the article.

- Look up the word *diaphragm* in the dictionary, and write the complete definition.

Warrior Bees

Bees are amazing. Perhaps you already know that honeybees pollinate more than 30 percent of all fruits and vegetables. But did you also know that armies in all ages have used bees in warfare?

In the first century B.C., the mighty army of Pompey the Great was advancing on Asia Minor (present-day Turkey). The people who lived there, called the Heptakometes, had to think fast. Somehow they had to outwit the Roman invaders. The plan they devised was based on two facts. They knew their bees were currently gathering pollen from rhododendron and azalea plants. That meant that the honey crop would be loaded with *alkaloids*—which are harmless to bees but toxic to humans. What did they do? They left a large supply of poisoned honey in the path of 1,000 Roman soldiers! Naturally, the Roman soldiers seized and consumed the honey. Soon, they became deathly ill. So Pompey's mighty army was in no shape to defend itself against the clever Heptakometes!

Bees went to war in medieval times as well. At that time, ambitious invaders set out to conquer any city or castle they wanted. So builders came up with many imaginative defensive features. Often, they incorporated beehives within a castle's walls. Straw hives were also kept on the tops of high city walls—an unwelcome surprise for any wall-climber! Just before a siege, Roman legions often catapulted portable beehives at enemy positions. When the hives smashed explosively, a sudden assault of angry bees distracted the enemy. Before they knew it, the Romans were on top of them.

COMPREHENSION: Number the events to show the order in which they happened.

_____ Heptakometes obtain honey from beehives.

_____ Roman soldiers become sick.

_____ Heptakometes defeat the Roman soldiers.

_____ Bees gather pollen.

_____ Roman soldiers eat the honey.

RECALLING DETAILS:

1. By what name is Asia Minor known today? _____

2. The pollen of what blooming plants contain *alkaloids*? _____

   _____

3. What leader led the attack on the Heptakometes? _____

   _____

Warrior Bees (page 2)

LOOK IT UP! Check a dictionary or encyclopedia for information.

1. The Roman Empire existed from

    a. 27 B.C. to A.D. 395.

    b. 200 B.C. to 300 B.C.

    c. A.D. 100 to A.D. 200.

2. Medieval times, also called the *Middle Ages*, lasted from about

    a. 500 B.C. to 1450 B.C.

    b. A.D. 1007 to A.D. 1500.

    c. A.D. 500 to A.D. 1450.

3. All bees are

    a. hairy insects with four wings.

    b. located in only certain parts of the world.

    c. covered with yellow and black stripes.

VOCABULARY: Complete the sentences with words from the article.

1. _____ is the yellow powder found in flowers.

2. A device called a _____ works like a slingshot.

3. Something _____ has been built in.

4. A building's _____ features protect the people inside.

5. To _____ something is to grab it or take it by force.

6. A toxic substance is _____.

7. You are _____ when your attention has been drawn away from your main task.

DRAWING CONCLUSIONS: Circle a letter.

1. Using bees in warfare is an example of

    a. high technology.

    b. primitive technology.

    c. nuclear armament.

2. The soldiers in Pompey's army probably

    a. feared the Heptakometes.

    b. hadn't eaten for days.

    c. outnumbered the Heptakometes.

PICK A PROJECT: Work on the back of this sheet.

● Think of another way bees could be used in warfare. Explain your idea.

● Draw a picture to illustrate an event described in the article.

The English Language: Facts and Figures

Following are some interesting statistics (information in the form of numbers) about the English language in the world today.

- There are approximately 3,000 languages spoken in the world today. English is the official language in 87 countries or territories.

- There are 616,500 words listed in the Oxford English Dictionary.

- The average English-speaking person actually recognizes about 10,000 to 20,000 words.

- Every year, approximately 5,000 new words are added to the English language.

What percentage of . . .

- the world's population now speaks English? 20%

- people in the European Union are fluent English-speakers? 75%

- non-native persons around the world are fluent English-speakers?.................................... 25%

- all the books in the world are printed in English?..................... 50%

- international telephone calls are made in English?.................. 52%

- radio programs are broadcast worldwide in English?................. 60%

- global e-mail is exchanged in English? 68%

- global computer text is stored in English? 70%

- international organizations use English exclusively?.............. 33%

- English words are borrowed from languages other than the original Anglo-Saxon? 75%

- English words are made from Latin word parts? 50%

- all English words used throughout history no longer exist?................................. 85%

- the average English-speaker's conversation is made up of the 737 most frequently used words? 96%

COMPREHENSION: Write **T** for *true* or **F** for *false*.

1. _____ Two of every 10 people in the world today speak English.

2. _____ New words are seldom added to the English language.

3. _____ There are more than one million words listed in the Oxford English Dictionary.

4. _____ Fewer than 1,000 words are used again and again in most English-speakers' conversations.

The English Language: Facts and Figures   (page 2)

5. _____ About three-fourths of English words come from Latin.

6. _____ More than half of all radio programs are broadcast in English.

7. _____ Much of the vocabulary in Shakespeare's time is probably not used today.

8. _____ Most English-speakers use only about one-thirtieth of all English words.

VOCABULARY: Write an *antonym* from the article for each word below.

1. *exceptional* / _____

2. *worldwide* / _____

3. *native* / _____

4. *exact* / _____

5. *boring* / _____

6. *reproduction* / _____

WORDS IN CONTEXT: Complete the sentences with words from the article.

1. The United Nations and the Red Cross are examples of _____

   organizations.

2. Spanish and French are among the 3,000 _____ spoken today.

3. Two ancient languages that are *not* spoken in the world today are

   _____ and _____.

LOOK IT UP! Write the dictionary definitions.

fluent: _____

_____

exclusive: _____

_____

PICK A PROJECT: Work on the back of this sheet.

- Write three English words that include **each** of these Latin roots: *corp, dict, aud,* and *volv* (12 words in all).

- Do you think the worldwide use of English is increasing or decreasing? Explain your answer.

Life in the Olden Days: 1910–1920

Although some homes had electric light in this decade, most didn't. People lit their houses with gas lights or kerosene lamps. Food was kept cold in iceboxes, not refrigerators. Every week or so, a man in a horsedrawn wagon would deliver a big block of ice to put inside the icebox. The ice wagon followed a regular route from house to house.

Many houses didn't have piped-in water. Instead, people had to fill a bucket at an outdoor well. The bathroom was an outhouse—a tiny wooden building that was usually behind the main house. Inside, a hole cut in a wooden board was the toilet seat. There were no electric washing machines, toasters, irons, or vacuum cleaners.

Bicycles were called "wheels," so children didn't "ride bikes"—they "went wheeling." The pogo stick, patented in 1919, became a popular toy. In winter, kids enjoyed coasting downhill on their Flexible Flyer sleds. Movies were very short, black and white, and without sound. As a movie was shown in the theater, someone played background music on a piano. If the action was fast, the music was fast. If the scene was romantic, a love song was played. Radio had been invented, but very few programs were broadcasted. Many hobbyists built their own crude radios called "crystal sets."

The Boy Scouts, Girl Scouts, and Campfire Girls were all started in this decade. Two of the popular songs were "Alexander's Ragtime Band" and "Oh, How I Hate to Get Up in the Morning." Two of the liveliest dances were the Turkey Trot and the Bunny Hug.

COMPREHENSION: Write **T** for *true* or **F** for *false*.

1. _____ This article describes life in the first decade of the twentieth century.

2. _____ Compared to today, modern conveniences were few.

3. _____ People used big blocks of ice to keep themselves cool.

4. _____ There was no such thing as technology in 1910.

5. _____ Most people had radios, but there weren't many programs.

6. _____ Many houses had indoor plumbing and electricity.

Life in the Olden Days: 1910–1920   (page 2)

DRAWING CONCLUSIONS

1. How do you think people dried their laundry at this time?

   _____

   _____

2. What chore had to be done *before* you could wash dishes or take a bath?

   _____

   _____

   _____

3. What items were *not* in use in this decade? Cross out three items.

fireplace	piano
power drill	plow
rolling pin	computer
laundromat	washtub

SYNONYMS: Draw a line to make each match.

1. **bucket**   a. primitive

2. **crude**   b. frigid

3. **cold**   c. pail

NOTING DETAILS: Circle a word.

1. Bicycles used to be called (wheelies / wheels).

2. The Flexible Flyer was a popular (sleigh / sled).

3. In most homes, (steam / gas) or (kerosene / oil) lit the lamps.

VOCABULARY: Complete the sentences with words from the article.

1. A _____ is an official government document granting an inventor the right to make and sell the invention.

2. Something _____ inspires strong, loving feelings.

3. A _____ is the usual course of travel taken.

PLEASE EXPLAIN

Why do you think hobbyists wanted to build crystal sets?

_____

_____

_____

PICK A PROJECT: Work on the back of this sheet.

- Describe your favorite radio program in three or four sentences.

- Tell something about your family members who lived in this time period.

The History of Gymnastics

Strong, healthy bodies were very important to the ancient Greeks. That's why, about 2,500 years ago, they built the first gymnasiums. They wanted special places set aside for exercising.

Greek boys spent hours at the gym every day. They dreamed of winning events at the Olympics—the great sports competition started by the Greeks in 776 B.C. The teenagers practiced many different kinds of exercises in the gym. They ran around the track, lifted weights, and climbed ropes. They threw the discus and the javelin. Jumping, tumbling, and wrestling were also part of their training program.

Then the Romans conquered the Greeks. For a while, the Romans kept the gyms open. They even added a new kind of exercise—a strenuous workout on a wooden horse. But later, in A.D. 394, the Roman Emperor Theodosius abolished the Olympics. Boys no longer trained in the gyms, so most of them were closed.

Gymnastic sports nearly disappeared for almost 1,500 years! Then in the 1800s, some men in Germany and the Scandinavian countries started a campaign. They believed that gymnastics should be part of education. They said that regular, vigorous exercise would make young people strong in mind and body. That idea grew in popularity. Some schools in other countries followed their lead. When the first modern Olympics were held in 1896, gymnastics made a comeback.

Today, gymnastics plays an important role in the sports world. The television coverage of Olympic competitions has attracted millions of fans all over the world. In America, about 500,000 young people are working hard to become the next gold-medal winner.

COMPREHENSION: Circle a letter.

1. The earliest Olympic events were
   a. boxing and archery.
   b. wrestling and running.
   c. swimming and ice skating.

2. The first Olympic Games were held
   a. about 2,000 years ago.
   b. almost 3,000 years ago.
   c. in the reign of Theodosius.

The History of Gymnastics   (page 2)

3. In the United States today, there are about

   a. a half-million young gymnasts.

   b. 50,000 gymnasiums.

   c. 500 gymnastics competitions.

NOTING DETAILS: Circle a word.

1. The physical fitness of teenage girls was (encouraged / ignored) by the ancient Greeks.

2. A (Greek / Roman) ruler abolished the Olympics.

3. The gymnasiums trained young Greeks for (physical / mental) achievement.

BEFORE OR AFTER? Circle a word.

1. Most gymnasiums were closed (before / after) 776 B.C.

2. The sport of gymnastics was revived (before / after) A.D. 1500.

3. The first gymnasiums were built (before / after) the Romans conquered the Greeks.

ANTONYMS: Draw a line to make each match.

1. **regular**   a. instituted

2. **abolished**   b. deleted

3. **added**   c. caught

4. **threw**   d. occasional

VOCABULARY: Complete the sentences with words from the article.

1. An _____ is a particular contest in a program of competition.

2. An _____ is a person who rules an empire.

3. A _____ is a match between rivals.

4. Something that has *vanished* can be said to have _____.

5. An athlete who has *practiced* for long hours can be said to have _____ well.

6. A _____ is round and flat, while a _____ looks like a spear.

7. _____ includes somersaults and handsprings.

8. Someone or something makes a _____ when it returns after a long absence.

PICK A PROJECT: Work on the back of this sheet.

• Name and describe three Scandinavian countries.

• Draw a picture of a *discus* and a *javelin*. (If you need help, check a dictionary or an encyclopedia.)

The Most Sociable Mammal

The prairie dog is a member of the ground-squirrel family. It got its name from the sound it makes—a shrill bark, much like that of a dog. Prairie dogs can be found in the western part of North America, from Canada in the north to Mexico in the south.

The prairie dog is a fat little animal—about a foot long. Its short, coarse fur is grayish brown. It has small beady eyes, strong stubby legs, pouched cheeks, and a short, flat tail. Its favorite foods are alfalfa and grain.

Considered the most sociable of all mammals, prairie dogs live together in a community. They build their homes by digging a tunnel straight down for 12 feet or more. At the bottom of the tunnel, they hollow out several rooms. One of these rooms is used only for sleeping and another is used only for storing food. At the entrance to its home,

the prairie dog builds a chimney of earth. Why? To keep water from getting into the tunnel. The prairie dog stays in its tunnel most of the winter. If its food runs out, a prairie dog simply builds itself another home.

In summer, all the prairie dogs gather together. If an enemy, such as a coyote, comes in sight, the little animals warn each other with loud chirps or barks. Then they dive into their underground homes, where they are out of danger. Other enemies of the prairie dog include the rattlesnake and the burrowing owl. These animals often invade the home of the prairie dog and eat its food and young.

COMPREHENSION: Write **T** for *true* or **F** for *false*.

1. _____ Prairie dogs usually sleep all summer.

2. _____ The prairie dog is related to the ground squirrel.

3. _____ More prairie dogs live in Florida than in any other state.

4. _____ A prairie dog's legs are quite strong for their size.

5. _____ A prairie dog's tunnel is deeper than the average room is high.

6. _____ Like an apartment, some rooms in a prairie dog's home have specific functions.

The Most Sociable Mammal (page 2)

DRAWING CONCLUSIONS

1. What effect might a hard rainstorm have on a prairie dog's tunnel?

_____

_____

2. Why are prairie dogs called "sociable" animals?

_____

_____

ANTONYMS: Draw a line to make each match.

1. **entrance**   a. hostile

2. **enemy**   b. wispy

3. **coarse**   c. ally

4. **sociable**   d. exit

SYNONYMS: Draw a line to make each match.

1. **entrance**   a. rough

2. **enemy**   b. portal

3. **coarse**   c. congenial

4. **sociable**   d. foe

NOTING DETAILS

1. According to the article, where can prairie dogs be found?

_____

_____

2. What three animals are enemies of the prairie dog?

• _____

• _____

• _____

VOCABULARY: Use words from the article to complete the sentences.

1. An animal's _____ are its *offspring*.

2. A _____ sound is high and sharp.

3. A _____ is a warm-blooded animal that nurses its young.

4. _____ eyes are small, round, and sparkling.

5. _____ is a purple-flowered plant with long deep roots.

6. A _____ is an underground passageway.

PICK A PROJECT: Work on the back of this sheet.

• Create a crossword puzzle, using at least six words from the article.

• Write two new titles for the article.

• Imagine that you're writing a children's picture book about a curious prairie dog. What would you name your main character?

Money in History

Money has taken different forms and shapes in different times and places. Here are some fascinating facts about money in the past.

  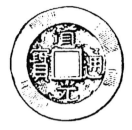 

- Until World War II, stone money was used on the Caroline Islands. The stones were round and had holes in the middle. Some pieces were so heavy they had to be strung on a pole and carried by two men.

- Between the years 1050 and 1108, one form of money used in France was made of leather.

- In Borneo, skulls were once used as money.

- The Chinese invented metal money nearly 4,000 years ago. At first they used gold cubes. Later, coins were made with holes in the middle so they could be carried on a string. These coins were called *cash*.

- Even today, the Masai in Africa consider cattle to be money.

- In ancient Greece, the *obol* was a tiny coin about the size of a pinhead. People carried obols in their mouths to keep them from getting lost.

- Some Native Americans cut clam shells into pieces to make money. They called it *wampum*. Since purple clam shells were harder to find, purple wampum was worth more than white wampum.

- *"Mind Your Own Business"* was engraved on the Franklin cent of 200 years ago.

- In the New Hebrides, feathers were once used for money.

- The first Chinese "folding money" was made of deerskin. Later it was made of paper. The larger the piece of paper, the more it was worth. One piece of paper, $8\frac{1}{2}$ by $13\frac{1}{2}$ inches, was worth 1,000 copper coins.

- At one time, money in England was made of wood.

- In 1685, when the government of Quebec was short of money, playing cards were used. The cards were cut into four parts and their value was written on them.

Money in History   (page 2)

COMPREHENSION: Write **T** for *true* or **F** for *false*.

1. _____ The *obol* was once a unit of money in Greece.

2. _____ At one time the Masai made coins from deerskin.

3. _____ About 200 years ago, the government of Quebec was short of money.

4. _____ White *wampum* had a greater value than purple *wampum*.

5. _____ Some French money was made of leather about 1,000 years ago.

NOTING DETAILS

1. What bit of good advice was once engraved on an American coin?

   _____

   _____

2. What unit of money mentioned was the smallest in size?

   _____

3. In Quebec, how many units of money were made from one playing card?

   _____

4. Where and why did people once carry coins in their mouths?

   _____

   _____

DRAWING CONCLUSIONS: Circle a letter.

1. Four thousand years ago, the date was approximately
   a. 200 B.C.
   b. 2000 B.C.
   c. A.D. 2000.

2. The Franklin cent described was minted in about
   a. 1802.   b. 1920.   c. 1776.

VOCABULARY

1. A _____ is one of the soft, light parts that grow out of the skin of birds.

2. The word _____ was first used to describe a kind of Chinese coin.

3. A _____ is the bony framework of the head.

4. A _____ is one kind of shellfish.

PICK A PROJECT: Work on the back of this sheet.

• Draw an illustration of a dollar bill. Include all the elements and make your drawing as exact as possible.

• Write the dictionary definition of *money*.

Wonderful Stevie

Stevie Wonder can do it all. He writes songs. He sings songs. And he plays the piano, drums, organ, and harmonica. For more than 40 years he has been thrilling audiences with magical displays of his talent.

Stevie's real name is Steve Judkins. In 1950, he was born blind in the state of Michigan. At age two, he tried to make music by pounding a tin pan with a spoon. His mother bought him a cardboard drum. After the drum came a little harmonica that had just four holes. Friends and family were amazed by the music he could make with only those four notes.

Stevie's family lived in a poor section of Detroit. He attended special classes for the blind at a public school there. At age 10, the "boy wonder" was entertaining people all around the neighborhood. Friends remember that he "played his voice" like a musical instrument. The music he liked best was rhythm and blues.

In 1960, Stevie was hired by Motown Records. Some executives there renamed him "Little Stevie Wonder." He had his first big hit, "Fingertips," at age 12. And he started going to a new school—the Michigan School for the Blind. There he learned to study music by using books and song sheets written in Braille. His career moved very fast. Among his numerous hit records are favorites like "Superstition" and "You Are the Sunshine of My Life."

Stevie's music never stops changing. He is always reaching out for new sounds. At any time, this master music-maker might feel inspired and start singing another hit song!

COMPREHENSION: Cross out information that is *not* in the article.

1. Stevie Wonder prefers to wear his hair in dreadlocks.

2. Stevie Wonder is a multi-talented performer.

3. Stevie's family name is Judkins.

4. Recording executives renamed him "Stevie, the Boy Wonder."

5. Stevie showed exceptional musical talent at any early age.

Wonderful Stevie   (page 2)

NOTING DETAILS

1. As a boy, Stevie Wonder lived in

   _____, _____.
         (CITY)   (STATE)

2. The kind of music he liked best was

   _____.

3. After Stevie learned

   _____, he studied

   books about music.

4. Because Stevie was _____,

   he attended special classes.

5. The four instruments Stevie can play

   are the _____,

   _____, _____,

   and _____.

CHARACTER STUDY: Circle three words to describe
Stevie Wonder.

wistful	innovative	unhappy
gifted	pretentious	female
mute	belligerent	admired

ANTONYMS: Write a word from the article to complete
each sentence.

1. _____ and *wealthy*

   are opposites.

2. To get *fired* is the opposite of getting

   _____.

DRAWING CONCLUSIONS: Circle a letter.

1. Stevie Wonder is now

   a. nearly 70 years old.

   b. over 50 years old.

   c. exactly 45 years old.

2. When Stevie was hired by Motown
   he was just

   a. 10 years old.

   b. 12 years old.

   c. eight years old.

3. Stevie Wonder's career spans four

   a. decades.

   b. generations.

   c. instruments.

SYNONYMS: Draw a line to make each match.

1. **displays**   a. part

2. **amazed**   b. exhibitions

3. **section**   c. employed

4. **hired**   d. astonished

PICK A PROJECT: Work on the back of this sheet.

● Name your favorite Stevie Wonder song
  and tell why you like it best.

● Write some lyrics (at least four lines)
  for your own song.

The Little Rascals

Have you ever watched any of the old black-and-white comedies called *The Little Rascals* on TV? From 1922 to 1944, 221 *Our Gang* movies were made. These funny little films were a huge success. Audiences loved characters like Alfalfa, with his squeaky voice; Darla, the "little sweetheart;" and Stymie, with his derby hat. Renamed *The Little Rascals* for telecasting, the old *Our Gang* shows are still very popular with children and adults alike.

What was it like for the child actors in the early days of films? The kids didn't have to memorize whole scripts. Instead, they were "fed" three or four lines at a time. It was okay for them to make up lines if the lines fitted in. If the kids did a good job of acting, they were rewarded with ice cream.

Life on the set wasn't all fun and games, however. One reason was that the kids competed for lines. If one kid made too many mistakes, his or her lines would be given to someone else! And all the child actors worked long hours while their friends at home were free to play.

On the other hand, the kids made good money and often had fun. The boy who played Stymie earned enough money to help support his 13 brothers and sisters. The comedians Laurel and Hardy often visited the *Our Gang* set, riding in a funny little car. Laurel wore a derby like Stymie's and helped the kids make mudpies. And the studio gave each *Our Gang* performer a wonderful present every Christmas. One year, Darla asked for a dollhouse. Instead, she got a completely furnished room-sized playhouse. She and her friends quickly turned it into a clubhouse.

COMPREHENSION: Write **T** for *true* or **F** for *false*.

1. _____ Abbott and Costello often played with the young cast members.

2. _____ The *Our Gang* movies were shot in living color.

3. _____ A character named Stymie wore a derby hat.

4. _____ Episodes of *Our Gang* have never been televised.

The Little Rascals (page 2)

NOTING DETAILS

1. A character named _____ was the gang's "little sweetheart."

2. What three compound words in the article end in *house*?

   • _____

   • _____

   • _____

3. A comedian named Stan Laurel made _____ with the child actors.

4. The salary of which character helped pay the bills for his very large family?

   _____

ANTONYMS: Draw a line to make each match.

1. **funny**   a. miniscule

2. **rewarded**   b. tragic

3. **huge**   c. blunders

4. **mistakes**   d. penalized

VOCABULARY: Circle a letter.

1. Characters' *lines* are
   a. places to stand on the stage.
   b. the words they speak.
   c. sketches for costumes.

2. *Alfalfa* is the name of
   a. a child actor.
   b. the creator of *Our Gang*.
   c. an *Our Gang* character.

3. *Movies* and *films* are
   a. antonyms.
   b. homonyms.
   c. synonyms.

BEFORE OR AFTER? Circle a word.

1. Audiences watched *The Little Rascals* (before / after) they watched *Our Gang*.

2. The cast members got ice cream (before / after) giving a good performance.

PLEASE EXPLAIN

How do you know that the same actors could not have appeared in *all* the *Our Gang* movies?

_____

_____

_____

_____

PICK A PROJECT: Work on the back of this sheet.

• Draw a picture of a *derby*. If you need help, look up "hats" in an encyclopedia.

• What would be good and bad about being a child actor? Explain your thinking.

The Bad Old Days of Basketball

Do you think modern basketball is a pretty rough game? In the old days—about 110 years ago—basketball was *very* rough. Many players wore padded pants, knee guards, and elbow pads. The stories that came out of the Pennsylvania coal towns were shocking. Before they came to watch a game, some miners heated nails with their mining lamps. When they didn't like what was happening on the court, they threw the hot nails at the players and referees. Some referees carried guns to protect themselves!

The small basketball courts of that time caused problems, too. The walls of the gym were the boundaries. That meant that both the balls and the players often bounced off the walls. Many players were pushed onto the stoves and radiators that were also within the boundaries. So burns were common basketball injuries.

Soon, bigger courts made room between the boundary lines and the walls. Now there was space to line up

chairs for fans. But when the ball went out of bounds, there was still trouble. Basketball rules were different then: The first player to touch the ball out of bounds got to throw it back into play. So the players often chased the ball out of bounds—racing right into the crowd. In the fight for the ball, fans and their chairs were knocked over. Some avid fans brought hatpins to the game. When an opposing player pushed up against them, they would stab him in the leg!

Looking back at the early days of basketball, today's players can be happy that times have changed.

COMPREHENSION: Write **T** for *true* or **F** for *false*.

1. _____ A century ago, basketball rules were different.

2. _____ The walls of the gym used to be the boundaries.

3. _____ Old-time fans liked to take an active part in the game.

4. _____ At one time, only sissies played basketball.

The Bad Old Days of Basketball   (page 2)

NOTING DETAILS

1. Name the two heating devices mentioned in the article.

   • _____

   • _____

2. What three kinds of protective gear were once worn by players?

   • _____

   • _____

   • _____

3. Name two common items that some fans used as weapons.

   • _____

   • _____

4. What is the only state mentioned in the article?

   • _____

SYNONYMS: Draw a line to make each match.

1. **avid**   a. regulations

2. **boundaries**   b. enthusiastic

3. **injuries**   c. ricocheted

4. **bounced**   d. borders

5. **rules**   e. wounds

VOCABULARY: Complete the sentences.

1. The word *gym* is short for

   _____.

2. The floor on which basketball is played is called a

   _____.

3. Those who are very interested in a sport are called _____.

4. _____ are the official rule-keepers in a basketball game.

ANTONYMS: Circle a word.

1. The opposite of a *common* injury is (*a usual / an extraordinary*) injury.

2. An antonym of *heated* is (*chilled / roasted*).

3. The opposite of *happy* is (*gratified / mournful*).

4. An antonym of *pushed* is (*shoved / pulled*).

PICK A PROJECT: Work on the back of this sheet.

• Do you think the early basketball players were professionals or amateurs? Explain your reasoning.

• Write two or three sentences describing some basketball injuries that are common today.

Krakatoa Erupts

In 1883, Krakatoa was a small island in the Indian Ocean. No one lived there. In May of that year, one of the three volcanoes on the island began to erupt. Within the next few months, the other two started erupting as well. Sailors at sea reported seeing a high cloud—some *six miles* high—over the island. They also heard explosions and saw flashes of light.

Then, on August 27, the entire island blew itself apart! The sound made was the loudest noise ever heard in history. It took four hours for that sound to reach Rodriguez, an island 3,000 miles away! The explosion shook the earth and made giant waves in the ocean. Called *tsunami*, these killer waves rose as high as 120 feet. They dumped billions of tons of water over the little islands around Krakatoa. Hundreds of villages were washed away, and 36,000 people were drowned.

Huge amounts of ash and bits of volcanic rock were thrown from the

erupting volcanoes. The wind blew tiny pieces of ash 50 miles into the sky. Red dust particles of ash continued to circle the world for two years, causing many blood-red sunsets.

When Krakatoa cooled off, a group of people went exploring the ruins there. They found that three-fourths of the island was gone, along with all the trees and plants. The explorers found just one living thing—a red spider, spinning a web.

The "big blow" at Krakatoa was probably the worst disaster ever caused by a volcano. Today, the island that was once Krakatoa is called *Anak Krakatoa*, meaning "child of Krakatoa."

COMPREHENSION: Write **T** for *true* or **F** for *false*.

1. _____ Giant, killer waves are called *tsunamis*.

2. _____ The eruption of Krakatoa was almost silent.

3. _____ Sailors saw a cloud hovering close to the island.

4. _____ There were three volcanoes on Krakatoa.

Krakatoa Erupts   (page 2)

NOTING DETAILS: Complete the sentences.

1. The last living thing on Krakatoa

   was a _____.

2. An _____ called

   Rodriguez is 3,000 miles away from

   Krakatoa.

3. Ash particles from the eruption circled

   the world for _____

   years.

4. Two kinds of debris hurled from the

   volcanoes were _____

   and _____.

DRAWING CONCLUSIONS: Circle a number.

1. The "big blow" at Krakatoa happened

   about (170 / 120) years ago.

2. Today, Krakatoa is about (one-fifth /

   one-fourth) its original size.

3. From beginning to end, the disaster at

   Krakatoa lasted about (3/10) months.

4. A billion is (1,000 / 10,000) millions.

5. A killer wave might be as tall

   as (20 / 30) six-foot men.

PLEASE EXPLAIN

Why didn't the volcano eruptions kill the
entire human population of Krakatoa?

_____

_____

_____

VOCABULARY: Circle a word.

1. The words *erupted* and
   (*oozed* / *exploded*) have similar
   meanings.

2. A synonym of *villages* is
   (*settlements* / *islands*).

3. The words *noise* and *sound* are
   (*antonyms* / *synonyms*).

4. A *disaster* might also be called a
   (*catastrophe* / *phenomenon*).

5. The words *particle* and (*part* / *speck*)
   have similar meanings.

6. A synonym of *shook* is
   (*squealed* / *trembled*).

PICK A PROJECT: Work on the back of this sheet.

• Look up *volcanoes* in an almanac or
  encyclopedia. Write two sentences each
  about three other famous volcanoes.

• Draw a picture of a *tsunami* about to
  engulf an island.

• Write another title for the article.

Some Sunny Facts

- The sun is colossal. It contains 99.8 percent of the total mass of the solar system.

- Even though the sun is huge, it is only about midway in the scale of star sizes. The bright red star Betelgeuse, for example, is a million times bigger than the sun.

- At its center, the sun is a hundred times more dense than water. The temperature at the sun's center is between 10 and 20 million° C.

- The pressure at the center of the sun is about 700 million tons per square inch. That's enough pressure to smash atoms, exposing the inner nuclei.

- How does the sun produce the radiation that gives off light and warmth? Radiation is caused by the interaction of atoms smashing into each other.

- The sun's total lifetime as a star capable of maintaining a life-bearing Earth is about 11 billion years. Half of that time has passed.

- It takes light from the sun about $8\frac{1}{2}$ minutes to reach the Earth.

- The sun moves in two ways. It rotates like a giant flaming top, completing each rotation in about 25 days. It also speeds ahead at about 43,000 miles per hour on its path through space. As it travels, it carries the Earth and all the rest of the solar system with it.

COMPREHENSION

1. What part of the sun is most dense?

   - _____

2. In what two ways does the sun move?

   - _____

   - _____

WORDS IN CONTEXT

1. What word in the article means "the amount of space inside something"?

   - _____

2. What word in the article means "energy created when changes take place in atoms"?

   - _____

Some Sunny Facts   (page 2)

NOTING DETAILS

1. How fast does the sun move as it travels through space?

   • _____

2. What star is a million times larger than the sun?

   • _____

3. What happens to atoms when they smash together?

   • _____

   _____

LOOK IT UP! Check a dictionary for information.

1. What is the **singular** form of the **plural** noun *nuclei*?

   • _____

2. Write the dictionary definition of the word *solar*.

   • _____

   _____

DRAWING CONCLUSIONS

1. Scientists say the sun can support life on Earth for another (11 / $5\frac{1}{2}$) billion years.

2. It takes (less / more) than 10 minutes for the sun's light to reach Earth.

3. Excluding the sun, all the planets in the solar system make up only (2 / .2) percent of its mass.

4. The abbreviation C. stands for (Centigrade / Circumference).

SYNONYMS: Draw a line to make each match.

1. **huge**   a. rotates

2. **middle**   b. colossal

3. **supporting**   c. center

4. **twirls**   d. maintaining

ANTONYMS: Write a word from the article next to its *opposite*.

1. *concealing* / _____

2. *dull* / _____

3. *beginning* / _____

PICK A PROJECT: Work on the back of this sheet.

• List four ways in which the sun supports life on Earth.

• Draw a simple picture of the solar system, showing the relationship of the planets to the sun.

• Make a simple crossword puzzle, using six words from the article.

Why Is English Hard to Learn?

Homographs are words with different meanings but exactly the same spellings. Words like these can cause a lot of trouble—especially for students studying English as a second language! Notice that each sentence below contains a pair of homographs.

1. Moe shed a tear when he saw the tear in his new shirt.

2. Rita's farmland was used to produce produce.

3. Why did Hector object to that object?

4. The invalid found that his insurance was invalid.

5. Will the soldier desert his platoon in the desert?

6. Which nurse wound the bandage around his wound?

7. The overfilled city dump had to refuse my refuse.

8. In such a strong wind, Kip couldn't wind the sail.

9. Will you intimate your secret to your intimate friend?

10. After a number of injections, Al's jaw got number.

11. When the does are present, the buck does strange things.

12. Is it time to present Lulu's birthday present?

13. The dove heard a noise and dove into the bushes.

14. Desperate for help, the farmer taught his sow to sow.

15. Don't subject me to more argument on that subject.

COMPREHENSION: Circle a word or words.

1. Homographs (are / are not) pronounced exactly alike.

2. Usually, homographs (are / are not) the same part of speech.

3. Most of the time, you (can / cannot) figure out the meaning of a homograph by using context clues.

Why Is English Hard to Learn?   (page 2)

COMPREHENSION: Write **T** for *true* or **F** for *false*.

1. _____ The words *by* and *buy* are homographs.

2. _____ The noun *dove* rhymes with the verb *dove*.

3. _____ The homographs *pitcher* and *pitcher* are both nouns.

VOCABULARY: Complete the sentences with words from the article.

1. The homograph _____ can mean "acts or performs" or "female deer."

2. The homograph _____ can mean "garbage" or "to reject."

3. The homograph _____ can mean "a female pig" or "to plant seeds."

4. The homograph _____ can mean "a gift" or "to give."

5. The homograph _____ can mean "a dry, sandy region" or "to abandon."

6. The homograph _____ can mean "an injury" or "wrapped or coiled around."

7. The homograph _____ can mean "to hint at something" or "very close."

8. The homograph _____ can mean "fruits and vegetables" or "to yield."

INFERENCE: Circle a letter.

1. In *homograph*, the word part *homo* must mean

   a. at home.   b. the same.   c. homely.

2. The word part *graph* must mean

   a. chart.   b. sound.   c. write.

COMPOUND WORDS: Complete the sentences with compound words from the article.

1. _____, meaning acreage used to raise crops, is a compound word.

2. You celebrate your _____ on the anniversary of the day you were born.

3. When something is crammed or loaded to its full capacity, we could say that it is _____.

LOOK IT UP! Write the dictionary definition .

1. *invalid* (noun): _____

   _____

2. *subject* (verb): _____

   _____

PICK A PROJECT: Work on the back of this sheet.

● Find another homograph in the first sentence (not *tear*). Write the two different meanings that word can have.

● Write original sentences using the homographs *bark, counter,* and *hide.*

Whatever Happened to the Passenger Pigeon?

The passenger pigeon is gone now. In 1914, the last of these beautiful birds died in the Cincinnati Zoo. Less than 200 years ago, people wouldn't have believed it. There were possibly *trillions* of passenger pigeons in eastern North America. Passenger pigeons, in fact, made up almost 40 percent of all birds in the United States!

In 1808, a scientist named Alexander Wilson reported seeing a huge flock in Kentucky. By his account, there were more than two and a half billion birds in that flock alone. He estimated the trail of birds in the sky to be 240 miles long.

In 1813, the famous ornithologist John James Audubon witnessed another amazing sight in Ohio. First he saw dark clouds moving at a startling rate about three miles away. Then he heard faint rumblings of thunder, which he thought was an approaching storm. But he noticed that the clouds were abnormally long and wide as they neared the great beech forest. Suddenly, the faint thunder became a roar, and a great vibration of air caused the ground to tremble! The clouds were alive—propelled by a billion wings flapping in unison. The passenger pigeons, on their annual flight southwest for the winter, were coming! The flock was so thick that it darkened the sun. It took three days for it to pass over the area.

Then people discovered that the passenger pigeon made good eating—and hunting began. During the nesting season, many railroad carloads of passenger pigeons were shipped to market each day. In New York and Chicago, the birds sold for one and two cents each. Because of the hunters' greed and foolish waste, the amazing passenger pigeon became extinct.

COMPREHENSION: Circle a word.

1. Passenger pigeons disappeared in the (19th / 20th) century.

2. Huge flocks of passenger pigeons were spotted in the (northern / eastern) United States.

Whatever Happened to the Passenger Pigeon? (page 2)

3. Most of the passenger pigeons were killed for (food / sport).

NOTING DETAILS

1. In what year did the last passenger pigeon die?

   • _____

2. In what direction did passenger pigeons fly for the winter?

   • _____

3. In what two cities were passenger pigeons sold for a few cents each?

   • _____

   • _____

4. In what two states did Wilson and Audubon sight passenger pigeons?

   • _____

   • _____

LOOK IT UP! Write the dictionary definition.

vibration: _____

_____

_____

COMPREHENSION: Circle a letter.

1. The words *witnessed* and *observed* are

   a. synonyms.   b. antonyms.

2. An *annual* event happens every

   a. other year.   b. 12 months.

3. You can barely hear a sound that is

   a. *distinct.*   b. *faint.*

4. An *abnormally* long cloud is

   a. *unusual.*   b. *commonplace.*

5. An *estimated* amount is

   a. *precise.*   b. *approximate.*

6. Animals or birds that feed or travel together are called a

   a. *flock.*   b. *flight.*

7. An *ornithologist* is a scientist who studies

   a. only pigeons.   b. birds.

PICK A PROJECT: Work on the back of this sheet.

• Look up *passenger pigeon* in an encyclopedia. Then write a description of that bird's color, size, etc.

• Do you think it really matters if an animal becomes extinct? Give reasons for your opinion.

Comparing Prehistoric Animals

Most people think of dinosaurs when they think of prehistoric animals. But some of the earliest creatures looked like animals that are still alive today. The oldest known fossils, for example, were formed by invertebrates—animals without backbones. Some of them resembled jellyfish, sponges, snails, clams, and worms. Others, of course, looked completely different from any of today's animals.

Here are some interesting facts about prehistoric animals:

- **Earliest known horse:** Called the *Eohippus*, this creature was about the size of a small dog.

- **Dinosaur eggs:** In 1923, scientists from the American Museum of Natural History first discovered dinosaur eggs in Mongolia.

- **Oldest known egg:** A primitive, mammal-like reptile laid this egg about 200 million years ago.

- **Largest flesh-eating animal:** The giant carnivore *Tyrannosaurus rex* stood almost 20 feet high and was about 45 feet long.

- **Earliest known bird:** Looking something like a dinosaur with feathers, the *Archaeopteryx* had teeth and a long tail.

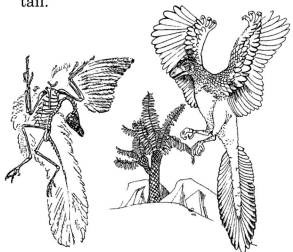

- **Largest four-footed animal:** *Brachiosaurus* weighed 50 tons and was about 80 feet long. It held its head 30 feet in the air.

- **Largest flying reptile:** The *Pteranodon* had a wingspread of 20 feet—about the length of a large car.

- **Longest neck:** The neck of the sea reptile *Elasmosaurus*, which contained 71 bones, was 25 feet in length.

- **Smallest dinosaur:** Having a skull only three inches long, *Compsognathus* was about the size of a chicken.

Some large groups of animals have nearly died out. Only a few survivors still remain on Earth. These creatures haven't changed much from their remote ancestors. They include the king crab, a relative of the scorpion, and the tuatara, a lizardlike reptile. Scientists call these creatures "living fossils."

NAME _____   DATE _____

Comparing Prehistoric Animals   (page 2)

COMPREHENSION: Write **T** for *true* or **F** for *false*.

1. _____ Mammals are the only animals that lay eggs.

2. _____ Dinosaurs lived millions of years ago.

3. _____ Worms and sponges are invertebrates.

4. _____ There was no such thing as a flying reptile.

5. _____ Fossils are the preserved remains of ancient creatures.

6. _____ All prehistoric creatures looked somewhat alike.

7. _____ The first discovery of a dinosaur egg occurred about 80 years ago.

DRAWING CONCLUSIONS: Circle a letter.

1. *Prehistoric* events happened
   a. before humans learned to write.
   b. about the time of the Roman Empire.
   c. when the first fossils were found.

2. The smallest dinosaur was
   a. the earliest known bird.
   b. called the *Pteranodon*.
   c. smaller than *Eohippus*.

3. *Brachiosaurus* was almost
   a. half the size of a small dog.
   b. twice as long as *Tyrannosaurus rex*.
   c. completely covered with feathers.

SYNONYMS: Draw a line to make each match.

1. **remote**   a. ancient

2. **backbones**   b. look like

3. **primitive**   c. spines

4. **resemble**   d. distant

LOOK IT UP! Check a dictionary or encyclopedia.

Where is Mongolia?_____

_____

_____

NOTING DETAILS

Name two "living fossils."

● _____

● _____

PICK A PROJECT: Work on the back of this sheet.

● Draw a picture of *Tyrannosaurus rex*.

● Did humans and dinosaurs live at the same time? Check an encyclopedia and write your answer.

Mailmen on Horseback

Daring horseback riders of the Pony Express once transported U.S. mail between St. Joseph, Missouri and Sacramento, California. If the mail was for residents of San Francisco, it was taken there by steamship.

From one station to the next, riders rode their mounts at top speed. As the rider approached a relay station, a fresh horse was brought out. The rider jumped from his horse, grabbed the mail bags, and was on his way in two minutes. Each man usually rode a distance of 75 miles. But if the next rider wasn't ready to go, the first rider kept going. There were about 100 stations, 400 station keepers, 400 horses, and 80 riders.

Pony Express riders rode day and night in all kinds of weather. They carried the mail in rainproof leather pouches strapped to the saddle. A load of mail never weighed more than 20 pounds. On short stretches, riders

occasionally made a speed of 25 miles per hour. They tried to move the mail about 250 miles per day.

The first Pony Express trip, in April of 1860, took 10 days to cover 1,966 miles. Later trips were made in eight or nine days. This was 12 to 14 days faster than the time it took for the Overland Mail, a stagecoach route, to cover the same distance.

The Pony Express ended in October 1861. Why? There was no need for it. That month the telegraph was finally extended all the way from coast to coast.

COMPREHENSION: Write **T** for *true* or **F** for *false*.

1. _____ St. Joseph, Missouri was the eastern end of the Pony Express route.

2. _____ Before the Pony Express, mail was carried by train.

3. _____ The first Pony Express trip took longer than later trips.

4. _____ Pony Express riders traveled all the way to San Francisco.

Mailmen on Horseback   (page 2)

NOTING DETAILS: Write words from the article.

1. The stagecoach service that delivered mail was called _____ _____.

2. At Sacramento, mail for San Francisco was loaded onto a _____.

DRAWING CONCLUSIONS

1. In all, how long did the Pony Express service last?

   • _____

2. The Pony Express route from Missouri to California covered about how many miles in all?

   • _____

3. In the Pony Express, what was the approximate ratio of horses to riders?

   • _____ to one

4. What invention made coast-to-coast communication much faster than the Pony Express?

   • _____

VOCABULARY: Circle a letter.

1. To *relay* something means to
   a. tell someone about it.
   b. take care of it.
   c. pass it on.

2. In the Pony Express, a *station* was a
   a. stopping place.
   b. broadcast studio.
   c. place to stand guard.

3. A *pouch* is a
   a. kind of strap.
   b. bag or sack.
   c. fancy purse.

4. The riders' *mounts* were their
   a. horses.
   b. saddles.
   c. mail bags.

HOMONYMS: Write words from the article that sound the same as the words below.

1. *male* / _____

2. *whether* / _____

3. *road* / _____

4. *knight* / _____

PICK A PROJECT: Work on the back of this sheet.

• Draw a picture of a Pony Express rider at full gallop.

• Give two reasons why Pony Express riders were thought to be "daring."

How Well Do You Know Your Body?

Consider these fascinating facts about the marvelous machine called the human body.

- Each square inch of human skin has about 19 million cells. On average, it also has 60 hairs, 90 oil glands, 19 feet of blood vessels, 625 sweat glands, and 19,000 sensory cells.

- Nerve signals may travel through nerve or muscle fibers at speeds as high as 200 miles per hour.

- Only one part of the human body has no blood supply. The cornea of the eye takes its oxygen directly from the air.

- You could live without 80 percent of your liver. Within a few months, a partial liver will reconstitute itself to its former size.

- The skin of the human body weighs six pounds.

- Sixty thousand miles of vessels carry blood to every part of the adult body.

- More than one million little tubes make up the human kidney. The total length of the tubes in both kidneys is about 40 miles.

- The human body has tiny bones once meant for a tail. It also has unworkable muscles once meant to move its ears.

- The hydrochloric acid of the human digestive system is highly corrosive. It can eat through a cotton handkerchief—and even through the iron of an automobile body! It does not endanger the walls of the stomach, however. The stomach is protected by a film of sticky mucus.

- About 80 percent of all body heat escapes through the head.

How Well Do You Know Your Body?   (page 2)

COMPREHENSION: Write **Y** for *yes* or **N** for *no*.

The article discusses . . .

1. _____ brain tissue

2. _____ skin glands

3. _____ blood vessels

4. _____ stomach acid

5. _____ the pancreas

6. _____ kidney tubes

NOTING DETAILS

1. What protects the walls of the stomach?

   • _____

2. What is the function of the blood vessels?

   • _____

   _____

3. What travels at 200 miles per hour?

   • _____

4. What body organ weighs about six pounds?

   • _____

5. How many hairs grow on a single square inch of skin?

   • _____

INFERENCE

Why should you wear a hat in cold weather?

_____

_____

LOOK IT UP! Write the dictionary definition.

cornea: _____

_____

VOCABULARY: Write a word from the article.

1. _____ are the basic units of living matter.

2. A _____ substance has the ability to eat into something else.

3. _____ is a thick, slimy substance made by the body.

4. An organ that can _____ itself can grow again.

PICK A PROJECT: Work on the back of this sheet.

• Look up *skin* in an encyclopedia. Copy the illustration showing a cross-section of the skin's layers.

• Explain the different functions of sweat glands and oil glands.

Produce: Is It Ripe? Is It Ready?

Do you know how to select the best fruits and vegetables at the grocery store? Are you a gardener looking for the ideal moment to harvest? Here are some tips about how and when to pick perfect produce.

CANTALOUPE Squeeze it gently. If it "gives" slightly and smells sweet, it's ripe.

PEACHES Pick when there is no green showing. For best flavor, let peaches ripen on the tree.

RASPBERRIES Pick berries when they loosen easily from the core. When the raspberries are fully ripe, the core will stay on the plant when you remove the fruit.

WATERMELONS Watermelons are ready to pick when the stem curls and turns brown. The part of the melon touching the ground should be yellow. Rap the melon with your knuckles and listen for a dull, hollow sound.

PEARS A ripe pear will have a faint yellow blush but still be greenish. Pears will get mealy if they're allowed to ripen on the tree.

PUMPKINS Pumpkins are ready when they turn deep orange and you can't penetrate their flesh with your thumbnail.

CORN Ripe corn will have a tight husk, and its silks will have dried and turned brown. Open an ear and stab a kernel with your fingernail. If the kernel contains milk, the corn is ripe. If the kerenel is tough and dry, it's overripe.

ASPARAGUS The tastiest stalks of asparagus are six to eight inches long and at least $1/2$ inch thick.

BROCCOLI Harvest when the buds (treetops) are dark blue-green and tightly closed. If the tops have begun to turn yellow, the broccoli was harvested too late.

BEANS Snap or string beans are best when they're as thick as a pencil. Seeds should not be visible through the pods. Lima bean pods should be a good green color and feel full.

POTATOES For mature potatoes—which will be the best keepers—harvest when the foliage has died down.

Produce: Is It Ripe? Is It Ready?   (page 2)

COMPREHENSION: Write **T** for *true* or **F** for *false*.

1. _____ Pears should ripen on the tree.

2. _____ Yellow broccoli is past its prime.

3. _____ Potatoes grow on stalks.

4. _____ Pick raspberries when the stems turn brown.

5. _____ Ripe corn has milky kernels.

6. _____ Rock-hard cantaloupes are not ripe.

NOTING DETAILS: Fill in the missing words.

1. _____ grow on a core.

2. The two melons mentioned are _____ and _____.

3. An ear of corn is wrapped in _____ and _____.

4. There is no _____ color on a ripe peach.

LOOK IT UP! Write the dictionary definition.

pod: _____

_____

VOCABULARY: Circle a letter.

1. Fruits and vegetables are called
   a. proteins.
   b. dietary supplements.
   c. produce.

2. *Mature* potatoes are
   a. thin-skinned.
   b. fully grown.
   c. slightly yellow.

3. *Foliage* is
   a. green and leafy.
   b. pods and seeds.
   c. sweet-smelling.

4. To *rap* something is to
   a. put it in a bag.
   b. knock on it sharply.
   c. shake it gently.

5. Something *mealy* is
   a. dry and crumbly.
   b. infested with bugs.
   c. soft and juicy.

6. A synonym of *harvest* is
   a. sow.   b. loosen   c. reap.

PICK A PROJECT: Work on the back of this sheet.

• Describe the look and taste of a perfect apple.

• Draw or describe an overripe banana.

Life in the Olden Days: 1920–1930

When World War I finally ended in 1919, Americans were ready to have some fun. Many people had more money than they had ever had before. Old-timers were shocked by the behavior of the young. Bold teenage girls and women had the nerve to bob their hair (cut it short). And their dresses were short, too; they actually showed the knees! The daring new dances, such as the Charleston and the Varsity Drag, were "sure to lead to trouble," according to many people.

Radio was becoming very popular. A favorite new show was *Grand Ole Opry*, featuring country music groups such as the Fruit Jar Drinkers and the Gully Jumpers. By 1926, sound came to the movies. Starring a newcomer named Mickey Mouse, *Steamboat Willie* was the first cartoon with a soundtrack.

Not all Americans were prosperous, however. Many children were working at hard jobs for long hours. Some children in New York tenements made tin toys and doll clothes—which were bought by the parents of rich kids. Other kids picked over dumps, looking for things to sell. On farms, kids worked from sunup to sundown ("can see" to "can't see"). In 1924, a child-labor amendment to the U.S. Constitution was proposed, but it failed to pass.

Model-T Fords were selling fast. They accounted for half the cars sold in 1920. Two million more were sold in 1923, and another two million in 1924. The first all-electric jukebox started blasting music in 1928. Other new inventions and discoveries included penicillin, Scotch tape, and Band-Aids. Among the most popular songs were "Yes, We Have No Bananas" and "Let a Smile Be Your Umbrella."

Then the stock market crashed in 1929. With that, the money was gone, and the good times came to an abrupt end.

Life in the Olden Days: 1920–1930   (page 2)

COMPREHENSION: Circle a letter.

1. The two major events that began and ended this decade were the

    a. end of World War I and the stock market crash.

    b. abolition of child labor and the beginning of radio.

    c. elections of Abraham Lincoln and Herbert Hoover.

2. In 1923 and 1924 combined, how many Model-T Fords were sold?

    a. 2 million

    b. 6 million

    c. 4 million

SYNONYMS: Draw a line to make each match.

1. **behavior**   a. shorten

2. **featuring**   b. scandalized

3. **bob**   c. conduct

4. **shocked**   d. starring

ANTONYMS: Complete the sentences with words from the article.

1. The opposite of _____ is *gradual*.

2. A _____ is the opposite of an *old-timer*.

3. *Sunup* and _____ are opposites.

NOTING DETAILS

1. A popular radio show of the decade was

    _____.

2. In the 1920s, the Charleston was a favorite _____.

3. The Gully Jumpers were a well-known

    _____.

4. The discovery of _____ gave sick people a way to fight infection.

5. In this decade, the American workforce legally included _____.

VOCABULARY: Complete the sentences with words from the article.

1. _____ are crowded old apartment houses, usually located in the slums.

2. An _____ is a change in or an addition to a bill, law, or constitution.

3. A _____ is a coin-operated record player.

PICK A PROJECT: Work on the back of this sheet.

- Create a crossword puzzle, using six words from the article. Be sure to write good clues.

- Why do you think the proposed child-labor amendment failed to pass? Explain your reasoning.

A President's First Speech

Until 1933, a newly elected president wasn't inaugurated until March 4. Then the 20th Amendment was passed. It made January 20 the day a new president and vice president took office. Although the date has been changed, new presidents still take the same oath of office that George Washington did. They promise "to preserve, protect, and defend the Constitution of the United States." Every inauguration day thousands of visitors flock to Washington, D.C. to hear the inaugural address.

This is the new president's first speech. Throughout our nation's history, presidents have used this speech to explain their goals. If the election was an especially bitter contest, they will often call for unity.

In 1800, when Thomas Jefferson became president, political parties were a new development. Some people were nervous. They feared that Jefferson would listen only to members of his own party. Members of the losing party didn't want to be ignored. But Jefferson calmed their fears by calling for "harmony and affection." He told his audience that "every difference of opinion is not a difference of principle."

"My fellow Americans, ask not what your country can do for you, but what you can do for your country."

In 1865, America was still torn by civil war. President Abraham Lincoln's call for unity was perhaps the most famous inaugural address. "With malice toward none," he said, "with charity for all . . . let us strive on to finish the work, to bind up the nation's wounds . . . to do all which may achieve and cherish a just and lasting peace among ourselves, and with all nations."

Another famous inaugural speech was delivered by Franklin Roosevelt in 1933. The country was suffering from the Great Depression. Roosevelt assured the nation that things would get better, and that "the only thing we have to fear is fear itself." President John F. Kennedy gave a stirring inaugural address in 1961. "My fellow Americans," Kennedy said, "ask not what your country can do for you, but what you can do for your country."

COMPREHENSION: Circle a word.

1. An inauguration speech is given at the (beginning / end) of a presidency.

2. The date of inauguration was changed by an amendment to the (Declaration of Independence / Constitution).

A President's First Speech   (page 2)

3. When (Lincoln / Jefferson) was elected, political parties were well established.

4. In (1961 / 1933), Franklin Roosevelt delivered a great inaugural speech.

5. On Inauguration Day, the new president takes the (address / oath) of office.

NOTING DETAILS

1. The names of how many U.S. presidents are mentioned in the article?

   • _____

2. Before 1933, on what date were U.S. presidents inaugurated?

   • _____

3. Does the article name Thomas Jefferson's political party?

   • _____

4. What was Abraham Lincoln talking about when he mentioned "the nation's wounds"?

   • _____

   _____

SYNONYMS

1. What three words quoted from the oath of office are *synonyms*?

   • _____

2. What word in the article is a synonym of *speech*?

   • _____

3. What word in the article is a synonym of *ill will* or *spite*?

   • _____

VOCABULARY: Complete the sentences with words from the article.

1. To _____ something is to hold it dear and treat it with love.

2. An _____ is a solemn promise to speak the truth.

3. Someone's _____ are that person's aims and purposes.

4. The condition of being in harmonious agreement is called _____.

DRAWING CONCLUSIONS

What do you think the weather is usually like on Inauguration Day?

_____

PICK A PROJECT: Work on the back of this sheet.

• Explain why people were fearful during the Great Depression.

• Write two lines for your own inaugural speech. Use your imagination.

Ancient Inventions

Their motive was simple: Prehistoric humans wanted to increase their control over the world around them. That's why they carved tools out of stone and made bows out of wood. It took less effort to shoot an arrow than it did to throw a spear. They also found it was easier—and more effective—to cross rivers and lakes on logs. A log raft allowed them to float rather than swim across water. But our ancient ancestors weren't satisfied. Next, they used fire to burn out the center of logs. Why? To make canoes!

No one knows when the first wheel appeared. But most historians believe the Sumerians invented wheeled wagons and chariots. These people lived about 3,500 years ago in Mesopotamia—now a part of modern Iraq. Mesopotamians and Egyptians invented the plow to increase their grain crops. They also invented metal tools to cut stone. As they acquired more knowledge of building methods, they developed the carpenter's level. The Sumerians also invented writing. And they learned to make papyrus reeds into a tough kind of paper.

Ancient Greeks discovered new technical arts when they traveled to

other lands. On returning home, some Greek travelers were greeted as the inventors of the tools they brought back! But Theodorus, a Greek artist who lived about 530 B.C., is thought to have actually invented the key and the lathe. And a Greek called Glaucos is credited with inventing a means of welding iron.

In ancient China, the process of making silk was probably developed before 2700 B.C. This was one of the most important Chinese inventions. Because silk cloth was important in world trade, the Chinese carefully guarded their silk-making secrets for thousands of years. About 800 A.D., the fine art of making porcelain originated in China. During the 1000s, the Chinese contributed to the development of gunpowder. They used the explosive primarily for rockets, grenades, and fireworks.

COMPREHENSION: Write **T** for *true* or **F** for *false*.

1. _____ Mesopotamia is now part of modern Iran.

2. _____ The Sumerians invented writing.

3. _____ Two ancient inventors' names are mentioned in this article.

Ancient Inventions   (page 2)

4. _____ The silk-making process was developed in the 1000s.

5. _____ Inventions from five ancient lands are mentioned in the article.

NOTING DETAILS: Circle a word.

1. Metal tools were invented so people could cut (stone / papyrus).

2. To increase their grain crops, Egyptians invented the (plow / wheel).

3. The key was invented by an ancient (Egyptian / Greek).

DRAWING CONCLUSIONS

What product did the Chinese trade for goods in other parts of the world?

_____

LOOK IT UP! Write the dictionary definition.

porcelain: _____

_____

_____

VOCABULARY: Complete the sentences with words from the article.

1. A _____ is a desire that makes a person want to do something.

2. A _____ cuts into and turns the soil.

3. A _____ is a machine used to cut and shape wood or metal.

4. _____ is a tall plant that grows in or near water in Egypt.

ANTONYMS: Draw a line to make each match.

1. **satisfied**   a. useless

2. **simple**   b. solid

3. **effective**   c. discontent

4. **hollow**   d. complex

BEFORE OR AFTER? Circle a word.

1. The year 530 B.C. came (before / after) the year 430 B.C.

2. The chariot was invented (before / after) the silk-making process.

3. The spear was invented (before / after) the bow and arrow.

PICK A PROJECT: Work on the back of this sheet.

- In your opinion, which was the most important invention mentioned in the article? Explain your thinking.

- Name three products made from grain crops.

Rules of Thumb

A rule of thumb is a kind of homemade recipe for making a guess. Rules of thumb are like tools. They can help you appraise a problem or situation. They can give you "a feel" for a subject. Rules of thumb are fascinating and usually easy to remember. But just how accurate are these folksy little guidelines? They fall somewhere between a mathematical formula and a shot in the dark!

Rules of thumb are different from other old-time sayings. A famous proverb, for example, says "a stitch in time saves nine." But a rule of thumb says "allow one inch of yarn for every stitch on a knitting needle." People's rules of thumb aren't always right. They're simply personal tools for making things work—most of the time, under most conditions.

Here are some interesting, informative, and amusing rules of thumb:

- **Tree Roots:** The diameter of a tree trunk in inches is the radius of the root system in feet.

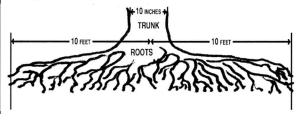

- **Keyboarding:** Two handwritten pages equals one typed page.

- **Buying a Hat:** Your ring size is likely to be the same as your hat size.

- **Cutting Firewood:** One person, working alone, can cut, haul, and stack a cord of firewood a day.

- **Feeding Livestock:** Two heifers eat as much as one cow; one cow eats as much as seven sheep.

- **Estimating Adult Height:** Your adult height will be twice your height at the age of two.

- **Using a Paint Roller:** The average paint roller will apply two to three square feet of paint per dip.

- **Heating with People:** Ten people will raise the temperature of a medium-size room one degree per hour.

- **Cooking Beans:** When cooked, eight quarts of dried beans will feed 100 people.

- **Planting Seeds:** Never plant a seed deeper than twice its width.

Rules of Thumb   (page 2)

COMPREHENSION: Circle a letter.

1. A rule of thumb is like

    a. a tool.

    b. a recipe.

    c. both a and b.

2. Someone's own rule of thumb comes from his or her

    a. exact measurements.

    b. personal experience.

    c. fantastic dreams.

3. Two dimensions are

    a. inches and feet.

    b. north and south.

    c. height and width.

DRAWING CONCLUSIONS: Write **P** for *proverb* or **RT** for *rule of thumb.*

1. _____ *When the cat's away, the mice will play.*

2. _____ *One ostrich egg provides breakfast for 24 people.*

3. _____ *Waste not, want not.*

4. _____ *One bushel of apples makes three gallons of cider.*

LOOK IT UP! Check a dictionary for information.

How long, wide, and high is a *cord* of firewood?

_____

_____

SYNONYMS OR ANTONYMS? Write **S** or **A**.

1. _____ conditions / circumstances

2. _____ recipe / formula

3. _____ twice / half

4. _____ identical / different

5. _____ informative / educational

VOCABULARY: Complete the sentences with words from the article.

1. Young cows that haven't given birth to a calf are called

    _____.

2. The _____ of a circle is a straight line passing through its center from side to side.

3. The _____ of a circle is a straight line extending from its center to its side.

4. The phrase _____

    _____ means

    a wild guess.

PICK A PROJECT: Work on the back of this sheet.

• Write one or two rules of thumb you or your family uses.

• Choose the rule of thumb from the article you think is *least* likely to be true. Explain why you think so.

   Reading Comprehension—Nonfiction 1 • © Saddleback Educational Publishing • www.sdlback.com

Life in the Olden Days: 1930–1940

The Great Depression lasted all through the 1930s. Business failed and so did the banks. Because people couldn't find work, millions of families were hungry. Many people stood in lines to get free soup and bread. When they couldn't come up with the rent or house payment, poverty stricken families were evicted from their homes.

Dust storms raged in mid-America. After years of drought, nothing would grow anymore. America's great farmlands were now called the *Dust Bowl*. Many farmers gave up and headed west, where they hoped for better luck. Thousands of families, with no homes and no jobs, were on the road. Hoping to find work, some hitched rides on freight trains heading for new places. Fortunately, government programs were started to help people get by until circumstances improved.

While still in high school, two boys named Jerry Seigel and Joseph Schuster created Superman. When the first *Superman* comic book was issued in 1938, the character was an instant hit. Other fictional newcomers that decade were Mary Poppins, Nancy Drew, Flash Gordon, and the first Dr. Seuss book for little children.

Big-band swing music was in, and the "King of Swing" was Benny Goodman. Besides swing, some other popular dances were the Susie Q and the Jitterbug. And thousands of people in the '30s sang along to songs such as "The Music Goes Round and Round" and "Three Little Fishies."

Parents were worried about what radio was doing to kids. In scary programs like *The Shadow*, a smashing melon was used as a sound effect for a head being bashed in. Some adults denounced radio as "blood-curdling bunk."

Life in the Olden Days: 1930–1940   (page 2)

COMPREHENSION: Circle a letter.

1. In the 1930s, large numbers of Americans

   a. suffered flood damage.

   b. went to bed hungry.

   c. worked long hours.

2. Flash Gordon and Nancy Drew were popular

   a. band singers.

   b. fictional characters.

   c. radio shows.

3. Millions of the homeless and hungry got some relief by means of

   a. government programs.

   b. individual citizens.

   c. moving to Europe.

4. The first *Superman* comic book hit the news stands about

   a. 55 years ago.

   b. 88 years ago.

   c. 65 years ago.

5. The Great Depression occurred

   a. in the decade following World War II.

   b. in the third decade of the twentieth century.

   c. in the same decade as the Civil War.

DRAWING CONCLUSIONS

In the 1930s, parts of Kansas, Texas, Oklahoma, New Mexico, and Colorado came to be known as the _____

_____.

FACT OR OPINION? Write **F** for *fact* or **O** for *opinion*.

1. _____ Americans suffered more in the 1930s than in any other decade.

2. _____ Charitable organizations provided meals to the hungry.

3. _____ In general, American business ground to a halt in the 1930s.

VOCABULARY: Complete the sentences with words from the article.

1. To be _____ is to be forced to move from a dwelling place.

2. A long period of dry weather, with little or no rain, is a _____.

3. If you have strongly spoken out against something, you have _____ it.

PICK A PROJECT: Work on the back of this sheet.

• Explain how you might make a "galloping horse" sound effect for a radio show.

• Write a descriptive title for this article.

NAME _____   DATE _____

What's a Geyser?

A *geyser* (**GY zer**) is a natural spring that throws up hot water with explosive force from time to time. Sometimes the water shoots up in great columns, cloudy with steam.

"Old Faithful" in Yellowstone National Park is probably the world's most famous geyser. On average, it erupts for about four minutes once every 65 minutes. On two occasions, its eruptions were only 33 minutes apart. The height of Old Faithful's eruptions is usually about 120 to 150 feet.

Many other geysers erupt at irregular intervals. No one knows when they will go off. Some erupt several times an hour. Others don't go off for hours, days, weeks, or even months. When some geysers erupt, the water bubbles only a few feet off the ground.

Geysers behave a lot like volcanoes. But volcanoes shoot forth melted rock, while geysers erupt water containing a solution of minerals. After an eruption, the water seeps back into the earth. Deposits of silica or lime carbonate are left behind. Often, these deposits take beautiful and curious forms. Many form cones. The "Giantess" in Yellowstone Park, for example, forms craters that fill with wonderfully clear water between eruptions. The mineral deposits left by other geysers look a lot like weird castles and towers.

There are at least 200 active geysers in Yellowstone Park. One, known as the "Giant," throws a column of water 175 feet into the air. Other well-known geysers are found in very different lands. One lies in Iceland, in the midst of barren lava fields. Here, about 70 miles from Reykjavik, the capital, dozens of geysers appear in a circle about 10 miles across. The other noted group of geysers is located far to the south. If you want to see them, you will have to travel to New Zealand—on the other side of the world!

COMPREHENSION: Write **T** for *true* or **F** for *false*.

1. _____ After a geyser erupts, the water quickly evaporates.

2. _____ Some geysers don't erupt for years at a time.

What's a Geyser? (page 2)

3. _____ Old Faithful erupts approximately every hour.

4. _____ Geysers exist in both the northern and southern hemispheres.

5. _____ After an eruption, deposits of sodium chloride are left behind.

6. _____ Teams of scientists build geysers for the public's enjoyment.

NOTING DETAILS

1. What geyser in Yellowstone Park leaves craters behind?

   • _____

2. How high in the air does "the Giant" throw water?

   • _____

3. What happens to erupted water that does not evaporate?

   • _____

   _____

4. How many active geysers are located in Yellowstone Park?

   • _____

LOOK IT UP! Check a dictionary for information.

Most of Yellowstone Park is located in what part of what state?

_____

SYNONYMS: Draw a line to make each match.

1. **craters**   a. treeless

2. **barren**   b. famous

3. **noted**   c. occasional

4. **irregular**   d. bowls

VOCABULARY: Complete the sentences with words from the article.

1. A _____ is the mixture made when something is dissolved in a liquid.

2. A flow of water from the ground is called a _____.

3. _____ are the gaps in time between happenings or events.

4. _____ are solid substances found in the earth that were never animal or vegetable.

5. _____ can also be called *water vapor*.

PICK A PROJECT: Work on the back of this sheet.

• Describe two important differences between geysers and volcanoes.

• Why do you think "Old Faithful" was given that name? Explain your thinking.

The History of Gliders

Humans' first successful flights with wings were made in gliders. In 1678, a French locksmith named Besnier made an amazing claim. He said that he flew from the rooftop of his house, using paddlelike wings on his shoulders and feet. But Besnier's boastful claim seemed unlikely, and he was never able to prove it.

In 1810, Sir George Cayley made the first biplane glider in England. With its wing surface of 300 square feet, it could glide a few yards while carrying a man. Next he built a larger glider that carried his coachman a distance of 900 feet before it crashed. While the coachman wasn't injured, he was so frightened that he quit his job.

Otto Lilienthal of Germany was the first to develop and fly successful gliders. Beginning in 1891, he made more than 2,000 glider flights. On one flight, he went 1,300 feet. In the United States, a Chicago man named Octave Chanute also developed some gliders in the 1890s. His gliders made many short flights from the sand dunes along Lake Michigan. Chanute, an engineer, added a number of steering devices controlled by cords. In earlier gliders, the pilot had to swing his feet and body from side to side to change direction. Chanute's rudders and ailerons enabled

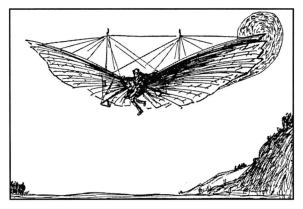

pilots to control the glider without so much body movement.

From 1900 to 1902, Wilbur and Orville Wright experimented with gliders at Kitty Hawk, North Carolina. Later, in 1911, Orville made what was probably the first soaring flight in a glider. The ride lasted almost 10 minutes!

Most people lost interest in gliders in the early 1900s. Why? The development of the powered airplane made gliding look tame. But gliding was revived by the Germans after World War I. By 1939 there were 186,000 German glider pilots. Larger gliders were built during World War II. They were used for transporting soldiers, field artillery, and even light tanks. These gliders did no soaring. They were towed from place to place by large airplanes. The Germans first used such gliders in the invasion of Belgium.

After World War II ended, glider enthusiasts devoted themselves to breaking records.

The History of Gliders   (page 2)

COMPREHENSION: Circle a word.

1. A glider is an airplane that can fly without (an engine / a tail).

2. A glider can (plummet / soar) upward on wind and heat currents.

3. In the early (19th / 20th) century, Orville Wright made a 10-minute glider flight.

4. Sir George Cayley made the first biplane glider in (Germany / England).

NOTING DETAILS

1. During World War II, gliders were used to carry what vehicles?

   • _____

2. How far did Sir George Cayley's best glider travel?

   • _____

3. A Frenchman named Besnier attached homemade wings to which body parts?

   • _____

4. How many years after Sir George Cayley's first glider flight did Orville Wright soar for 10 minutes?

   • _____

LOOK IT UP! Write the dictionary definition.

ailerons:_____

_____

YOUR OPINION, PLEASE

Would you have enjoyed being an employee of Sir George Cayley? Why or why not?

_____

_____

VOCABULARY: Complete the sentences with words from the article.

1. A _____ is a hinged, vertical flap at the rear of an aircraft, used for steering.

2. Something is said to be _____ when it is brought back to life or returned to popularity.

3. _____ is the name used for large, mounted guns, such as cannons.

4. You are _____ goods when you carry them from one place to another.

5. Those who have a great interest in something are called _____.

PICK A PROJECT: Work on the back of this sheet.

• Explain why the huge gliders used in World War II "did no soaring."

• How do you think it feels to float through the air in a glider? Use your imagination to describe the experience.

Clouds, Clouds, and More Clouds!

As any cloud-watcher knows, all clouds are not alike. Some clouds are great fleecy masses, like piles of fluffy cotton. Some are feathery streamers high in the sky. Others are dull gray or black sheets that hint at rain. But in one way clouds are all the same. Every cloud is made up of condensed water vapor, composed of either tiny drops of water or ice crystals.

Scientists who study clouds have given them Latin names. The four main forms of clouds are *cirrus, stratus, nimbus,* and *cumulus.* Each name describes the cloud's appearance.

Cirrus means "curl" or "ringlet of hair." These are curly white clouds made of ice crystals. You can see them high above all other clouds. Some cirrus clouds rise five or 10 miles above the earth's surface.

Stratus, which means "spread out," is a large, foglike cloud. These clouds usually form very near the earth. They are often seen in the early morning or late evening when the air is still.

Cumulus, the Latin word for "heap," describes the heaped-up masses of white clouds you see in summer. These clouds increase in size and number when the sun is warmest in mid-afternoon.

Nimbus is the name the Romans gave to the dark gray rain cloud. A nimbus is a rather shapeless cloud formation. Its lower half is heavy with moisture, which turns into falling raindrops.

Many clouds are classified according to height. *Alto-cumulus* clouds are white or grayish cumulus clouds packed closely together. They occur at heights of 8,000 to 20,000 feet. *Alto-stratus* is a thick cloud sheet of gray-blue that appears from 6,500 to 20,000 feet above ground. *Cirro-stratus* is a thin white sheet formed of ice crystals. *Cirro-cumulus* is a mass of small cumulus clouds. These last two cloud forms appear at heights above 20,000 feet.

Clouds, Clouds, and More Clouds!   (page 2)

COMPREHENSION: Circle a letter.

1. What kind of clouds are likely to float across the sky on a warm summer day?

   a. nimbus   b. stratus   c. cumulus

2. Three forms of water mentioned in the article are

   a. stratus, cumulus, cirrus.

   b. vapor, drops, crystals.

   c. hot, cold, warm.

3. The four major cloud forms are named for their

   a. looks.   b. weight.   c. color.

DRAWING CONCLUSIONS: Circle a word.

1. The prefix *alto-* must mean (high / low).

2. Clouds formed of ice crystals must be (higher / lower) than clouds made of water droplets.

NOTING DETAILS

1. Which clouds are closest to the earth?

   • _____

2. Which clouds are farthest from the earth's surface?

   • _____

3. Which two classifications of clouds appear at heights above 20,000 feet?

   • _____

   • _____

ANTONYMS: Write words from the article that have *opposite* meanings.

1. *depths* / _____

2. *shapely* / _____

3. *winter* / _____

4. *shiny* / _____

5. *late* / _____

6. *rarely* / _____

SYNONYMS: Write words from the article that have the *same* meanings.

1. *piles* / _____

2. *primary* / _____

3. *curl* / _____

4. *arranged* / _____

5. *quiet* / _____

PICK A PROJECT: Work on the back of this sheet.

• Draw the four main forms of clouds. For help, use the descriptions in the article.

• Make a crossword puzzle, using six words from the article. Make sure your clues are clear.

• Write a different title for the article.

Proverbs: Wisdom in a Nutshell

A proverb is a bit of practical wisdom handed down from generation to generation. Proverbs from all around the world show that people everywhere share common experiences and values. The following proverbs are only a tiny sample of old folk sayings that still qualify as good advice.

FRIENDSHIP

1. *One old friend is better than two new ones.* (RUSSIAN)

2. *Tell me who your friends are, and I'll tell you who you are.* (PHILIPPINE)

3. *Choose your friends like your books, few but choice.* (ENGLISH)

4. *A near friend is better than a far-dwelling kinsman.* (ENGLISH)

5. *Correct your friend secretly and praise him publicly.* (CZECH)

6. *A fair-weather friend changes with the wind.* (SPANISH)

WORK

7. *A bad workman blames his tools.* (AFRICAN)

8. *To the spectator, no work is too hard.* (GERMAN)

9. *Without work in summer, without boots in winter.* (POLISH)

10. *Fine work is its own flattery.* (SLOVAKIAN)

TIME

11. *Wasting time is robbing oneself.* (ESTONIAN)

12. *Time flies as fast as a shuttle on the loom.* (VIETNAMESE)

13. *To those who know how to wait, everything comes in time.* (FRENCH)

14. *Time heals a wound, but leaves a scar.* (MEXICAN)

15. *What may be done at any time will be done at no time.* (ENGLISH)

16. *Time brings out the truth better than a judge.* (HUNGARIAN)

Proverbs: Wisdom in a Nutshell   (page 2)

COMPREHENSION: Write **T** for *true* or **F** for *false*.

1. _____ The proverbs in the article are arranged in three categories.

2. _____ Proverbs from 16 nations are included in the article.

3. _____ A people's proverbs reflect their insights and observations.

4. _____ "Different strokes for different folks" is a modern American proverb.

5. _____ The ideas behind many proverbs are still applicable in today's technological world.

MATCHING MEANINGS: Write the number of a proverb in the article.

1. "Have few friends though many acquaintances" is similar to proverb no. _____.

2. Proverb no. _____ and "Birds of a feather flock together" express the same idea.

3. Proverb no. _____ means the same as "The work praises the workman."

SYNONYMS: Draw a line to make each match.

1. **relative**   a. spectator

2. **select**   b. kinsman

3. **watcher**   c. wound

4. **injury**   d. choose

ANTONYMS: Write words from the article.

1. The *antonyms* in proverb no. 5 are _____ and _____.

2. In proverb no. 9, two words with opposite meanings are _____ and _____.

VOCABULARY: Complete the sentences with words from the article.

1. _____ is good judgment that comes from knowledge and experience in life.

2. _____ advice is both sensible and useful.

3. _____ is excessive praise that may not be sincere.

4. When you _____ someone, you point out his or her mistakes.

5. A _____ is a machine for weaving thread or yarn into cloth.

PICK A PROJECT: Work on the back of this sheet.

• Explain the meaning of "fair-weather friend." Give an example.

• Give two reasons why old friends may have more value than new friends.

• Paraphrase (restate in your own words) the idea behind proverb no. 7.

The Terrifying Tomato

Probably no other garden product has as many uses as the tomato. A fruit used as a vegetable, the juicy red tomato is one of the best sources of vitamins A and C. The tomato is now one of the most important greenhouse food crops and the number one garden product canned in the United States. Yet tomatoes weren't always a basic part of our diet.

The tomato was introduced to Europe when Spanish explorers brought it back from Central America in the 1500s. It became quite popular then—but only for a while. For some reason, people decided that the tomato was poisonous. The rumors were terrifying. Some people came to believe that if they ate a tomato, they'd be dead before midnight! Why? No one knows for sure. It may have been because the tomato is a member of the nightshade family—which includes many poisonous plants. From that time on, Europeans grew tomatoes only for decoration.

Early colonists brought tomato seeds to Virginia and grew them in their flower gardens. Thomas Jefferson was one of the first Americans to eat tomatoes. Then, in 1820, the great tomato scare finally came to an end. On September 26, a man in Salem, Oregon made an impressive demonstration. As hundreds of people watched, he stood on the courthouse steps and ate a whole basket of tomatoes! He didn't die. He didn't even get sick.

Most Americans, however, didn't eat tomatoes until sometime after the Civil War. Then people went to the other extreme. They decided that tomatoes were a medicine! A product called Dr. Miles's Compound Extract of Tomato was sold throughout the United States. It was guaranteed to cure anything that ailed you. Today, we still use a tomato product that's very like Dr. Miles's Compound—but we call it catsup.

COMPREHENSION: Cross out information that does *not* appear in the article.

1. The tomato is related to the potato, pepper, and eggplant.

2. The tomato is classified as a fruit.

3. More tomatoes are canned than any other garden product.

4. Tomato juice contains acid.

The Terrifying Tomato   (page 2)

NOTING DETAILS

1. Explorers from what country brought tomato seeds to Europe?

   • _____

2. Who was one of the first Americans to eat tomatoes?

   • _____

3. Tomatoes are members of what "suspicious" family of plants?

   • _____

4. What old-fashioned "medicine" was made from tomatoes?

   • _____

   _____

5. What important vitamins do tomatoes provide?   • _____

DRAWING CONCLUSIONS: Circle a number.

1. Most Americans didn't start eating tomatoes until after (1945 / 1865).

2. Tomatoes were brought to Europe about (500 / 750) years ago.

3. Thomas Jefferson lived in the (18th and 19th / 17th and 18th) centuries.

SYNONYMS: Write a word from the article next to its synonyms.

1. favored, beloved, _____

2. toxic, deadly, _____

3. scary, frightening, _____

4. hearsay, gossip, _____

ANTONYMS: Draw a line to make each match.

1. **noon**   a. best
2. **eliminates**   b. sold
3. **laughable**   c. midnight
4. **bought**   d. impressive
5. **worst**   e. includes

VOCABULARY: Complete the sentences with words from the article.

1. A _____ is a building with a glass roof and sides that can be heated in cold weather.

2. The _____ of something is its wellspring or origin.

3. The early European settlers in America were called _____.

4. Law trials are held in a

   _____.

LOOK IT UP! Check a dictionary for information.

Another acceptable spelling of *catsup* is _____.

PICK A PROJECT: Work on the back of this sheet.

• Name three common dishes that are made from tomatoes.

• Name two or three popular varieties of tomatoes.

A Story Behind Every Word

As every student of *etymology* knows, word histories can be fascinating. Here are the interesting "past lives" of some words you see and hear all the time.

● BLOCKBUSTER

We're always eager to see a movie or read a book described as a *blockbuster*. The original blockbuster, however, was a bomb used during World War II. How did it get its name? Its explosive force was so great that it could level an entire city block! Before long, people started using that word to describe anything that made a spectacular impact.

● MASCOT

Do your school's sports teams have a lucky *mascot*? In 1880, an opera called *La Mascotte* premiered in Paris. Titled after a provincial word for "witch," this opera featured an extremely lucky central character. Thereafter, the word *mascot* came to mean any person or object that brought good fortune.

● SNIPER

Hunters in medieval England found it difficult to snag a quick and wary bird called the *snipe*. They finally learned to hide themselves and take the speedy snipe by surprise. Today, we use the word *sniper* for any solitary marksman who shoots from a place of concealment.

● BIGWIG

How can you tell if someone is a *bigwig* or just an ordinary guy? In old England, a powdered sheepskin wig was the hallmark of a judge. Clearly, a man who could decide the fate of others was a man of great importance! Over time, anyone in a position of authority came to be called a *bigwig*.

● HAMSTRUNG

Have you ever been *hamstrung* by a difficult problem? Long ago, butchers discovered that the tendons in a ham are vital to a pig's movements. When hamstrings were accidentally or deliberately cut, the animal couldn't walk or run. Today, anyone who is rendered incapable of getting on with something might be called *hamstrung*.

A Story Behind Every Word   (page 2)

COMPREHENSION: Write **T** for *true* or **F** for *false*.

1. _____ A *mascot* is an important person of authority.

2. _____ A *sniper* tries to ambush his prey.

3. _____ The president of the United States is a *bigwig*.

4. _____ An airplane pilot might be *hamstrung* by bad weather.

NOTING DETAILS

1. What word in the article was first used by butchers?

   • _____

2. What word is based on the name of a bird?

   • _____

3. What word is spelled differently today than it was in the 19th century?

   • _____

4. Which two words in the article originated in England?

   • _____

   • _____

WORD ANALYSIS

1. Which three words in the article are *compound words*?

   • _____

   • _____

   • _____

2. Which of the five key words in the article *cannot* be used as a noun?

   • _____

VOCABULARY: Complete the sentences with words from the article.

1. The words *alert* and _____ are synonyms.

2. A _____ is addressed as "Your honor."

3. Something that existed or happened in the Middle Ages (A.D. 500–1450) is described as _____.

4. The words *destiny* and _____ are synonyms.

5. The words *accidentally* and _____ are antonyms.

6. _____ is the study of words and their origins.

LOOK IT UP! Write the dictionary definition.

hallmark: _____

_____

PICK A PROJECT: Work on the back of this sheet.

• Copy the word history of *hamburger* from the dictionary.

• Describe a *blockbuster* book or movie.

Two Unusual Pirates

In the 1600s and 1700s, the waters of the Caribbean were favorite haunts for pirates. Rich merchant ships were ripe for plunder. And there were plenty of islands in this part of the Atlantic. The islands' lonely bays were perfect places to anchor—safe from the hangman's noose!

Except as captives, women were seldom found on pirate ships. Yet there were a few female pirates—such as Anne Bonney and Mary Read. Pictures show them dressed as men and armed to the teeth. No one doubted that they were as tough as their male shipmates!

Anne Bonney was the high-spirited but dutiful daughter of a rich plantation owner—until she met John Rackham. Handsome and rich, "Calico Jack," as he was called, was also a daredevil pirate. Not surprisingly, Anne's father objected to the match. So Anne disguised herself in sailor's clothes, and the lovestruck couple sailed away. On Rackham's pirate ship, Anne met Mary Read, another female pirate dressed as a man.

Unlike Anne, Mary had grown up poor in England. Before joining Rackham's crew, she had run away from home and fought as a soldier in France. She was known to be fiercely expert with both the cutlass and the pistol.

In the fall of 1720, the governor of Jamaica sent out an armed sloop to capture Rackham and his crew. All the pirates fled below decks—except Anne and Mary. The two women fought gallantly and were the last two to be taken prisoner. The whole crew was tried and convicted of piracy on November 28, 1720. Mary was sentenced to hang—but before that could happen, she died of a fever. Anne's execution was postponed, and her ultimate fate is still unknown. On the day that Rackham was hanged, however, she was still angry about his cowardly behavior under attack. "If you had fought like a man," she is reported to have said, "you need not have been hanged like a dog."

Two Unusual Pirates   (page 2)

COMPREHENSION: Circle a letter.

1. What was the main idea of the article?

   a. Anne Bonney and Mary Read died young.

   b. Pirates once roamed the Caribbean.

   c. Not all pirates were men.

2. The two female pirates came from

   a. similar backgrounds.

   b. dissimilar backgrounds.

   c. England and Ireland.

3. About how many years ago did the events in the article happen?

   a. 150   b. 300   c. 500

4. Why did pirates attack merchant ships?

   a. to capture their sailors.

   b. to protest their government.

   c. to steal their cargo.

LOOK IT UP! For information, check an atlas or a map.

Off which coast of the United States is the Caribbean located?

_____

DRAWING CONCLUSIONS

1. What symbolic drawing appeared on a pirate flag?

   ● _____

2. What country mentioned in the article is on an island in the West Indies?

   ● _____

SYNONYMS: Write words from the article next to their *synonyms.*

1. _____ / *hangouts*

2. _____ / *prisoners*

3. _____ / *robbery*

4. _____ / *executioner*

VOCABULARY: Complete the sentences with words from the article.

1. The words *often* and

   _____ are antonyms.

2. Someone called a

   _____ is bold and

   reckless.

3. A _____ is a short, curved sword with one sharp edge.

4. A _____ is a small sailboat with one mast, a mainsail, and a jib.

5. When something is

   _____, it is put off until

   a later time.

6. A *buccaneer* is the same thing as a

   _____.

PICK A PROJECT: Work on the back of this sheet.

● Draw a pirate flag.

● Describe two unusual jobs that some women do today.

Life in the Olden Days: 1940–1950

World War II dominated every American's thoughts from 1941 to 1945. Air raid drills were held. Black curtains were draped over windows so enemy bombers couldn't spot towns by their lights. More and more mothers worked outside the home to "help the war effort." The nation's economy improved. Scarce things like sugar, coffee, meat, and gasoline were rationed. People were issued a limited number of stamps that could be traded for goods. Each person, for example, was allowed to buy two pairs of shoes a year.

People planted Victory Gardens to grow vegetables in vacant lots. Rubber, paper, and aluminum were in short supply. So children collected anything made of these materials for recycling.

After the war, life returned to normal on the homefront. The word *teenager* became part of the language. For the first time, young people from 13 to 19 years old were designated as a special group. Saddle shoes and huge "Sloppy Joe" sweaters were popular fashions for both boys and girls. In the late 1940s, teenage girls also started wearing blue jeans and men's shirts.

Some popular expressions of the decade were *What's cookin', good-lookin'?*;

Long time no see; and *Hubba-hubba*. Money was *moolah*, and a snappy dresser looked *nifty*.

Juvenile Jury, a radio show in which children from five to 11 years old offered advice about problems, was all the rage. Another favorite radio program was *Quiz Kids*. On this show, smart kids answered tough questions that would stump most adults.

A skinny young singer named Frank Sinatra was making girls scream, swoon, and faint. "Nature Boy" and "Mairzy Doats" were two of the decade's top hits.

Life in the Olden Days: 1940–1950   (page 2)

COMPREHENSION: Circle a letter.

1. Some of the items *rationed* during World War II were
   a. jet planes and helicopters.
   b. carrots, potatoes, and corn.
   c. shoes, gas, and sugar.

2. Some items that children might collect for recycling were
   a. worn out tires and cooking pots.
   b. leftover food and milk.
   c. clippings from trees and bushes.

3. Two of the most popular radio shows of the decade
   a. were broadcast late at night.
   b. featured panels of children.
   c. starred Frank Sinatra.

4. Americans fought in World War II for
   a. 5 years.
   b. 10 years.
   c. 4 years.

COMPARING PAST AND PRESENT

In the 1940s, *moolah* and *nifty* were commonly used expressions. What expressions used today have the same meanings?

- _____

- _____

VOCABULARY: Complete the sentences with words from the article.

1. The words *permitted* and _____ are synonyms.

2. When people share the same very important concern, their minds are _____ by that thought.

3. The words _____ and *occupied* are antonyms.

4. A *scrawny* person might also be called _____.

5. The words _____ and *styles* are synonyms.

6. You can _____ your opponent if you ask a question that she can't answer.

7. In the 1940s, a new term pointed out, or _____, teenagers as a special group.

8. Americans participated in *practices* called air raid _____.

PICK A PROJECT: Work on the back of this sheet.

- Compare 1940s fashions with today's favorite clothing styles.

- In what ways were the 1940s easier for Americans than the 1930s? In what ways were they harder?

The Last of its Kind

The first reptiles walked the earth about 300 million years ago. As the eons passed, these early creatures flourished and branched out. In effect, the first reptiles gradually turned into *many* kinds of animals. Scientists say that the first birds probably developed from certain reptiles. They also believe that other reptiles developed into the first mammals.

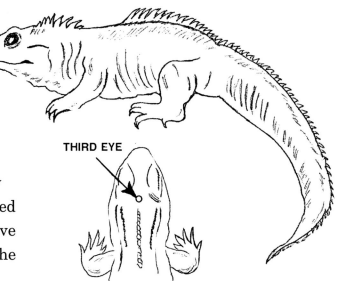

THIRD EYE

Reptiles themselves developed along many separate lines. Huge dinosaurs, flying reptiles, and reptiles of the sea spread throughout the earth in great numbers. Scientists now can identify 6,000 kinds of reptiles.

There are four main groups of reptiles living today. The first group—the largest of the reptiles—includes alligators and crocodiles. Members of this group have long bodies, tough skin, strong jaws, and powerful tails.

The second group is made up of turtles and tortoises. Their bodies are almost completely enclosed in hard, two-layered shells. When threatened, a turtle can find safety by withdrawing completely into this shell.

The third group is made up of lizards and snakes. No doubt you know that snakes are legless—but did you know they can't shut their eyes? Lizards, on the other hand, have four legs and are able to close their eyes.

The fourth group contains only one kind of animal—the *tuatara*. This strange creature looks somewhat like a lizard. It has three eyes (as many lizards do). But the tuatara's third eye, located on the top of its head, is covered by a thin layer of skin. It does not function as a normal eye, and no one knows what its function is. The tuatara can remain active at 52°F—a temperature at which most reptiles move about slowly, if at all. Scientists have a theory about the tuatara. They believe it is the last remaining member of a reptile group that was once widespread. Today the tuatara can be found only on islands off the coast of New Zealand.

The Last of Its Kind (page 2)

COMPREHENSION: Write T for *true* or F for *false*.

1. _____ Dinosaurs were reptiles.

2. _____ Scientists have organized reptiles into six categories.

3. _____ The tuatara cannot be found in North America.

4. _____ Turtles and snakes make up one of the main reptile groups.

5. _____ Every reptile has slimy skin.

6. _____ All of today's reptiles either creep or crawl.

NOTING DETAILS: Circle a word.

1. (Lizards / Crocodiles) have very strong tails.

2. Reptiles stop moving when the weather gets too (hot / cold).

3. Alligators are among the (largest / smallest) of the reptiles.

4. The tuatara's third eye is on its (back / head).

DRAWING CONCLUSIONS

Circle three words that could describe the *tuatara*.

friendly   unique   mammoth

coldblooded   extinct   scaly

LOOK IT UP! Write the dictionary definition.

theory: _____

_____

SYNONYMS: Draw a line to make each match.

1. **creatures**   a. thrived
2. **function**   b. operate
3. **identify**   c. recognize
4. **flourished**   d. security
5. **safety**   e. beings
6. **skin**   f. evolved
7. **developed**   g. hide

ANTONYMS: Write a word from the article next to its *opposite*.

1. *abruptly* / _____

2. *protected* / _____

3. *passive* / _____

4. *late* / _____

PICK A PROJECT: Work on the back of this sheet.

- Draw a picture of any two reptiles (except the tuatara) mentioned in the article.

- Explain the main difference between *turtles* and *tortoises*. Check an encyclopedia for information.

Devoted Daddies

Nurturing the young is usually the job of the female parent. But not always. "Dad" is the primary caretaker in many families. Even in the animal world, there are some especially faithful fathers.

• JACANAS

Sometimes these robin-sized wading birds are called "lily trotters." Can you guess why? Their long toes allow them to walk around on lily pads! Female jacanas are brightly colored and aggressive. The males are small, drab, and peaceable. After mating, the male incubates and tends the eggs for two weeks.

• ARROW POISON FROGS

You can find these vividly colored orange, red, and yellow frogs in South American rain forests. Females deposit their fertilized eggs on the backs of the males. After that, the males carry them until the eggs hatch and the tadpoles swim away.

• MARMOSETS

These squirrel-sized monkeys live in the dense jungles of South America. Typically, females give birth to twins.

After birth, the babies are carried through the trees by the male. He relinquishes them to the mother only very briefly—for nursing. When the combined weight of the twins equals his own, the male stops carrying them.

• MALLEE FOWL

These Australian birds are about the size of turkeys. The female lays her eggs in a large pile of decaying vegetation. From then on, the male tends the eggs alone. Every day he determines their temperature. Then he adjusts the compost pile to make sure the eggs are neither too hot nor too cold.

• RHEAS

Relatives of the ostrich, these large, flightless birds live in South America. A group of females deposit from 20 to 50

fertilized eggs in the nest of one male. That male incubates the eggs by himself. What are the females doing while Dad is at work? They've moved on to look for other males and other nests!

NAME _____ DATE _____

COMPREHENSION

1. Which three animals mentioned in the article don't fly?
   - _____
   - _____
   - _____

2. The male of which animal makes a nest? • _____

3. Which three animals live on the same continent? Which continent is that?
   - _____
   - _____
   - _____
   - _____

4. Which animal is the most colorful?
   - _____

5. Which animal is related to the ostrich?
   - _____

6. Which is the smallest bird described in the article?
   - _____

7. The young of which animal are called *tadpoles*?
   - _____

NOTING DETAILS: Circle a word.

1. Jacanas' long (legs / toes) enable them to walk on lily pads.

2. Mallee fowl are approximately the same size as (chickens / turkeys).

3. Marmosets leap through the trees of a (rain forest / jungle).

4. The female (jacana / rhea) is described as *aggressive*.

VOCABULARY: Complete the sentences with words from the article.

1. A _____ parent feeds and cares for its young.

2. The words *faithful* and _____ are synonyms.

3. To _____ an egg is to keep it warm and protected so it can hatch.

4. Rotting vegetable matter used to fertilize soil is called _____.

5. A parent _____ its offspring by letting it go.

6. *Places* and _____ are synonyms.

ANTONYMS: Write a word from the article next to its *opposite*.

1. *timid* / _____
2. *colorful* / _____
3. *male* / _____
4. *endlessly* / _____
5. *secondary* / _____

PICK A PROJECT: Work on the back of this sheet.

- Are male dogs and cats "faithful fathers"? Explain why or why not.

- In humans, which child-rearing tasks can best be done by a mother? Which can best be done by a father? Give reasons for your opinions.

Ever Seen a Falling Star?

A *meteor* is a piece of metallic or stony matter that hurtles into the Earth's atmosphere from outer space. More commonly called "shooting stars," meteors aren't visible until they plunge through our atmosphere. Most meteors never get that far. Those larger than dust particles are usually vaporized before they get close to Earth's surface. The average meteor is estimated to weigh only 0.0005 ounce!

Scientists suspect that as many as 200 million visible meteors enter the earth's atmosphere every day. The fastest meteors travel about 94,000 miles an hour as they speed around the sun. When meteors meet the Earth's atmosphere head-on, the combined velocity reaches about 160,000 miles an hour!

Meteors become visible when they're about 65 miles above the Earth. On almost any clear night, you can see some meteors for yourself. The trick is to get as far as you can from bright lights. If you have an unobstructed view of the sky, you can usually observe about six or seven meteors an hour. Don't go meteor-watching, however, when the moon is full or the moonlight is bright. These conditions will generally obliterate all but the brightest of meteors. Meteors rarely blaze for more than a few seconds. But sometimes a meteor leaves a shining trail that may last several minutes. Most of the meteors we see are no larger than a pinhead or a grain of sand.

What happens when Earth's orbit intersects a meteor stream? A "meteor shower" occurs, and the sky appears to be filled with flying sparks. But these displays of heavenly fireworks are very rare. At most, they occur only several times per century.

Meteors that reach Earth before burning up are called *meteorites*. In 1908, an enormous meteorite crashed to earth in Siberia. Estimated at a few hundred tons, this meteorite flattened forests like matchsticks and scorched a 20-mile area around the point where it hit. On impact, it exploded into fragments that left more than 200 craters.

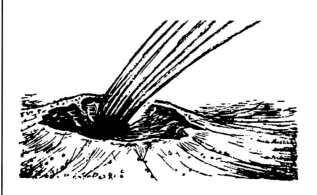

Ever Seen a Falling Star? (page 2)

COMPREHENSION: Write **T** for *true* or **F** for *false*.

1. _____ You can see more meteors when the moon is full.

2. _____ Most meteors are tiny.

3. _____ Meteor showers only occur during the winter months.

4. _____ Like comets, meteors are composed of dust and frozen gases.

5. _____ Meteors that don't vaporize before impact are called *meteorites*.

NOTING DETAILS: Circle a word.

1. We can't see meteors until they (enter / exit) Earth's atmosphere.

2. The average meteor can be observed for a few (minutes / seconds).

3. When a meteorite hits the Earth, it usually (explodes / collapses).

4. (Meteors / Meteorites) are sometimes called "falling stars."

LOOK IT UP! Write the dictionary definition.

meteorology: _____

_____

_____

DRAWING CONCLUSIONS

1. How do you know that meteors are part of our solar system?

   ● _____

2. About how many years ago did a meteor hit Siberia?

   ● _____

SYNONYMS: Write a word from the article next to its synonym.

1. *burned* / _____

2. *brilliant* / _____

3. *watch* / _____

4. *speed* / _____

VOCABULARY: Complete the sentences with words from the article.

1. The words *illuminate* and

   _____ are

   antonyms.

2. When a liquid or a solid is

   _____, it turns

   into a gas.

3. If nothing blocks your line of sight,

   your view is _____.

4. Solids, liquids, and gases are the three

   forms of _____.

DRAWING CONCLUSIONS: Circle three words that describe meteors.

frigid	swift	planetary
bright	mysterious	solid

PICK A PROJECT: Work on the back of this sheet.

● Explain the difference between a *meteor* and an *asteroid*. Check a dictionary for help.

● Draw a picture of a falling star.

World Heritage Sites

UNESCO, the United Nations Educational, Scientific, and Cultural Organization, has named the following national parks as World Heritage Sites. Which park interests *you* the most?

CARLSBAD CAVERNS NATIONAL PARK (New Mexico)

This is a network of more than 80 limestone caves, including the nation's deepest—1,597 feet. The Lechuguilla Cave is particularly noteworthy for its beautiful stalactites and stalagmites.

EVERGLADES NATIONAL PARK (Florida)

Here, a freshwater river six inches deep and 50 miles wide forms what the Seminoles called a "river of grass." Alligators, manatees, and Florida panthers make their home in the Everglades.

GLACIER BAY NATIONAL PARK (Alaska)

Made up of a huge chain of enormous tidewater glaciers, this park features a dramatic range of landscapes. Its animal population includes seals, bears, eagles, mountain goats, and whales.

GRAND CANYON NATIONAL PARK (Arizona)

When the Earth shifted about 65 million years ago, a huge area of land was lifted one and a half miles above sea level. For the last 6 to 10 million years, the Colorado River has been slowly carving the Grand Canyon down through the center of that land area.

MAMMOTH CAVE NATIONAL PARK (Kentucky)

This, the world's most extensive cave system, contains 345 miles of passages.

Rare animals such as blind fish and colorless spiders demonstrate adaptation to absolute darkness and isolation.

OLYMPIC NATIONAL PARK (Washington)

Snow-capped Mount Olympus is here, as are alpine meadows and glaciers. One of the world's few temperate rain forests is here as well. This rain forest is the result of warm, moist air from the Pacific meeting the mountains.

TAOS PUEBLO (New Mexico)

Built about 1400 B.C., *Pueblo de Taos* is the best preserved pueblo (Native American communal housing) in the United States. Still an active community, Taos is inhabited today by the Taos Pueblo Indians.

YOSEMITE NATIONAL PARK (California)

Located in the Sierra Nevada Mountains, this park features breathtaking scenery and a huge variety of plant and animal life. Its peaks, cliffs, monoliths, and domes were gouged and shaped during the last Ice Age.

World Heritage Sites   (page 2)

COMPREHENSION: Circle a word.

1. Mammoth Cave National Park is in
   (Kentucky / New Mexico).

2. A rare temperate rain forest is located
   in (Florida / Washington).

3. The (Pueblo / Seminole) Indians called
   the Everglades a "river of grass."

4. You could see glaciers in (one / two)
   of the national parks described.

5. The Grand Canyon is (older / newer)
   than the Taos Pueblo.

6. Glacier Bay National Park is in
   (Canada / Alaska).

NOTING DETAILS

1. What cave is famous for its gorgeous
   stalagmites and stalactites?

   ● _____

2. What river flows through the
   Grand Canyon?

   ● _____

3. In what mountain range is Yosemite
   National Park located?

   ● _____

4. What ocean's breezes helped to create
   a temperate rain forest?

   ● _____

DRAWING CONCLUSIONS

1. About how many years ago was Pueblo
   de Taos founded?

   ● _____

2. In what park would you be most likely
   to see colorful strata, or layers, of
   rock?

   ● _____

VOCABULARY: Complete the sentences with words
from the article.

1. _____ hang from a

   cave roof and _____

   build up from the cave's floor.

2. A _____ is a slow

   moving mass of ice and snow.

3. A very large block of stone may be

   called a _____.

4. A fish's gills are examples of an

   _____

   to its underwater world.

5. A series of connected caves make

   up a _____.

6. A _____ climate

   is neither very hot nor very cold.

PICK A PROJECT: Work on the back of this sheet.

● Draw pictures of two animals that
  live in the Everglades.

● Using at least six words from the
  article, create a crossword puzzle.
  Be sure to write good clues!

Life in the Olden Days: 1950–1960

Television came into its own in the 1950s. In February of 1950, there were three million TV sets in the United States. By the end of the year there were seven million sets—and by 1960, *50 million* sets! A study in 1951 showed that some junior high students were spending nearly 30 hours a week watching TV. The frozen TV dinner made its debut in 1954. Beginning in the mid-fifties, *Davy Crockett* became the hottest new TV series. Suddenly, kids everywhere begged for coonskin caps and Davy Crockett lunchboxes. *Howdy Doody* and *Captain Kangaroo* were also favorites of young audiences.

Many families moved out of cities and into the suburbs. There, young people often led tightly scheduled lives. More and more took dancing or piano lessons. Many also played in Little League baseball games and attended Scout meetings. Kids had more money to spend than they had ever had before. In 1953, a survey showed that kids spent most of their money on junk food. Some experts began to say that American kids were spoiled.

Teenage girls were going crazy over Elvis Presley. His first movie, *Love Me Tender*, hit the theaters in 1956. Without question, Elvis was the biggest of the 1950s rock stars. And rock 'n' roll was *big* then.

Disneyland opened its doors in 1955, *Mad* magazine cost 10 cents, and plastic hula hoops were a craze. Pegged pants and motorcycle jackets were popular clothing styles for boys. Girls favored pedal pushers and poodle haircuts.

People who weren't "with it" were called *squares*. And when a not-so-funny joke was told, the unamused listener might say *"Har-de-har-har."*

Life in the Olden Days: 1950–1960   (page 2)

COMPREHENSION: Circle a word or number.

1. During the 1950s, (music / television) was the newest thing in home entertainment.

2. In 1960, there were nearly (17 / 15) times more TV sets in America than there were in 1950.

3. (Girls / Boys) wore pegged pants in the 1950s.

4. The new musical sensation of the 1950s was (punk rock / rock 'n' roll).

NOTING DETAILS

1. American kids loved to watch TV shows starring _____ Crockett, Captain _____, and Howdy _____.

2. _____, America's first major theme park, opened in 1955.

FACT OR OPINION? Write **F** for *fact* or **O** for *opinion*.

1. _____ Children were spoiled by their parents in the 1950s.

2. _____ Boy Scouts builds character better than Little League does.

3. _____ Elvis Presley was the most popular and successful of all the rock 'n' roll stars.

VOCABULARY: Complete the sentences with words from the article.

1. Foods that have lots of calories but little nutrition are often called _____ _____.

2. _____ are neighborhoods on the outskirts of a city.

3. Something is said to make its _____ when it appears for the first time.

4. _____ caps were made from the hides of raccoons.

5. A _____ of children includes all those who were born at about the same time.

6. A _____ is a detailed study made by gathering and analyzing facts.

7. Davy Crockett's image was a popular illustration on the _____ kids carried to school.

PICK A PROJECT: Work on the back of this sheet.

● Interview a family member who was a teenager in the 1950s. Write two memories that person shares with you.

● Write two or three sentences about Davy Crockett. For information, check an encyclopedia.

The World's Oldest Stories

Just like us, ancient peoples were curious. But unlike us, they didn't have books to tell them what they wanted to know. So they made up their own answers. Over time, they wove these answers into some of the most imaginative and interesting stories the world has ever known. They reasoned, for example, that an object as wonderful as the sun must be more than human. So they made the sun a god. But they doubted that even a god could walk across the enormous sky between morning and evening. So they gave the sun a chariot drawn by magnificent white horses!

In time, such stories explained almost everything in nature. The rustling of the leaves must be the murmuring voice of the goddess who lived in the tree. The rushing stream must be a nymph hurrying to join her lover, the sea. And what about the stars? They must be good people the gods had placed in the sky so their virtues would never be forgotten.

These stories, called *myths*, are strangely similar in very different parts of the world. Some Native American

myths are like the stories told by the Romans. And some myths that grew up in Greece and Egypt are very much the same as Norse myths. How could this happen? Most scholars point out that even though ancient peoples lived in different places, they all lived in the same world. Because the same things were going on around them, it was natural for them to ask the same questions and come up with similar answers.

The whole system of these ancient stories is called *mythology*. When you study this subject, you will notice that there are two kinds of myths. *Explanatory* myths answer natural questions about natural objects. *Aesthetic* myths seem to have no object but to entertain.

COMPREHENSION: Write **T** for *true* or **F** for *false*.

1. _____ Only the Greeks and Romans created myths.

2. _____ The purpose of many myths is to explain natural events.

3. _____ Norse myths grew up in places like Sweden and Greenland.

4. _____ Ancient peoples from different places asked different questions.

The World's Oldest Stories   (page 2)

5. _____ Because myths are literally not true, no one studies them now.

6. _____ The study of myths is called *mythology*.

LOOK IT UP! Write the dictionary definitions.

*legend:*_____

_____

_____

_____

*myth:*_____

_____

_____

_____

DRAWING CONCLUSIONS

Explain the difference between a *myth* and a *legend*.

• _____

_____

ANTONYMS: Write a word from the article next to its *opposite*.

1. *teeny* / _____

2. *question* / _____

3. *artificial* / _____

4. *evening* / _____

5. *terrible* / _____

6. *remembered* / _____

VOCABULARY: Complete the sentences with words from the article.

1. Serious and accomplished students are called _____.

2. A _____ is a beautiful nature goddess who lives in trees or woods.

3. _____ are good moral qualities.

4. The word _____ describes something artistic or beautiful.

5. A _____ is an ancient, two-wheeled cart drawn by horses.

6. A _____ sound is low, soft, and steady.

SYNONYMS: Draw a line to make each match.

1. **alike**   a. magnificent

2. **inquisitive**   b. reasoned

3. **splendid**   c. curious

4. **thought**   d. similar

PICK A PROJECT: Work on the back of this sheet.

• What did the gods *Zeus* and *Jupiter* have in common? Get information from a dictionary or encyclopedia.

• Make up a myth explaining the sound of thunder. Write at least four or five sentences.

The Oldest Living Things

The giant sequoia tree ranks among the largest and oldest living things on Earth. Millions of years ago these trees grew in large forests throughout much of the world. Today, the giant sequoia grows only on the western slopes of the Sierra Nevada Mountains in California. The remaining giant sequoia groves range in area from just a few acres to a few square miles.

Many of the giant sequoias are several thousand years old. Nature has made them very durable, and they have no known enemies. None of these trees has ever been known to die from disease or insect attack. Lightning, however, has destroyed the tops of most of the largest giant sequoias.

Giant sequoias don't grow as tall as redwood trees, but their trunks are much larger. Several sequoias are about 100 feet around at the base. The diameter of the widest trunk is 37.3 feet.

In spite of its size, however, this mammoth evergreen is practically

useless as timber. Its wood is very brittle. When a tree falls, it often cracks both vertically and horizontally. The fragments are sometimes used to make lead pencils.

The tiny seeds—about one-quarter of an inch in size—take two years to mature. And the tree itself takes from 175 to 200 years to flower for the first time. This is the most delayed sexual maturity in all of nature.

COMPREHENSION: Circle a word.

1. (Sequoias / Redwoods) are taller than (sequoias / redwoods).

2. Some giant sequoias have been alive for (millions / thousands) of years.

3. Sequoias have no natural (enemies / seeds).

4. It takes sequoias (more / less) than 100 years to produce seeds.

The Oldest Living Things   (page 2)

5. The (diameter / circumference) of a sequoia trunk may be 100 feet.

6. Sequoias reproduce very (slowly / quickly).

DRAWING CONCLUSIONS

1. About how many sequoia seeds would fit in one inch of space?

   • _____

2. Why can't you buy sequoia wood in the lumber yard?

   • _____

3. Do sequoias drop their leaves in winter? How do you know?

   • _____

NOTING DETAILS

1. What two "health advantages" do sequoias have over most other trees?

   • _____

   _____

2. Where would you have to go to see a giant sequoia?

   • _____

   _____

3. What natural phenomenon has damaged many sequoias?

   • _____

VOCABULARY: Complete the sentences with words from the article.

1. _____ are small groups of trees without undergrowth.

2. A _____ is a kind of sickness or illness.

3. _____ are parts of something that have broken away.

4. An _____ of land covers 43,560 square feet.

5. *Lumber* and _____ are synonyms.

ANTONYMS: Draw a line to make each match.

1. **eastern**   a. western

2. **spongy**   b. horizontally

3. **vertically**   c. durable

4. **flimsy**   d. brittle

PICK A PROJECT: Work on the back of this sheet.

• Look at a map of California. Tell whether the Sierra Nevadas are in the eastern or western part of the state.

• Look up *sequoia* in an encyclopedia. Write two additional facts about these giant trees.

Baseball: The Changing Game

An old English game called *rounders* was the first form of the game we now know as baseball. In rounders, players ran in the opposite direction than base-runners do today. Then the English made some changes in the way rounders was played. In 1744, the rules for the new game, called *base-ball*, were published. In the early 1800s, Americans took up the game, changing the name to *townball*. In townball, there were no set fielding positions, and there were 20 or more players on each team!

The first set of standard baseball rules was written in 1845 by members of the Knickerbocker Base Ball Club of New York. The first organized baseball game was held on June 19, 1846 at the Elysian Fields in Hoboken, New Jersey. By 1900, baseball was played almost exactly as it is today.

Major league baseball has come a long way from that first game at Elysian Fields—and it is still changing. During the 1960s and 1970s, for example, the following changes occurred:

- Ten new teams were created—including two in Canada. (In 1993, two more teams—the Colorado Rockies and the Florida Marlins—joined the National League.)

- In 1965, the Houston Astros became the first team to play its home games in a domed stadium: the Astrodome. (Five big league stadiums now have domes or a roof that can be opened and closed.)

- The Astrodome was the first stadium to cover its field with plastic grass called AstroTurf. (Now there are 10 stadiums with artificial turf.)

- Speedy base runners and fielders became more important. Why? Because balls roll faster and bounce higher on artificial turf.

- In 1973, American League teams began using a "designated hitter" to take the pitcher's regular turn at bat.

- In 1975, players won the right to be "free agents." That allowed them to leave their teams when their contracts ran out and join other teams for more money. Free agency caused players' salaries to skyrocket.

Baseball: The Changing Game   (page 2)

COMPREHENSION: Cross out facts that are *not* in the article.

1. Baseball games were broadcast over the radio in the 1920s.

2. The 1960s and 1970s were a time of great growth in major league baseball.

3. Major league teams start spring training in February and March.

4. Organized baseball in America got started on the east coast.

NOTING DETAILS

1. In what city do the Astros play?

   ● _____

2. How does artificial turf affect the movement of the ball?

   ● _____

   _____

3. What name did the English give to the new game they created from *rounders*?

   ● _____

4. In what park was the first organized baseball game in America played?

   ● _____

DRAWING CONCLUSIONS

1. Do you think it's easier or harder to hit a home run in a domed stadium?

   ● _____

2. How do you know there were no centerfielders in the game of townball?

   ● _____

   _____

3. Standard baseball rules were written in America about how many years after base-ball rules were published in England?

   ● _____

SYNONYMS: Draw a line to make each match.

1. **ballpark**   a. speedy
2. **manmade**   b. stadium
3. **fast**   c. players
4. **teammates**   d. artificial

LOOK IT UP! Write the dictionary definition.

*Elysian fields:*_____

_____

_____

VOCABULARY: Complete the sentences with words from the reading.

1. When prices go up, up, and up they are said to _____.

2. _____ are written agreements that are legally binding.

3. *Minor* and _____ are antonyms.

PICK A PROJECT: Work on the back of this sheet.

● Write the names of the two major league ball clubs in Canada. Check an almanac if you need help.

● Do you think free agency is good or bad for baseball? Explain your thinking.

The Platypus

Have you ever seen a platypus? This odd animal—sometimes called a *duckbill*—lives alongside streams in Australia and Tasmania.

When zoologists examined a platypus for the first time, some thought it was a hoax. They suspected that parts of different animals had been sewed together! What's so unusual about this small insect-eater from "down under"? It has the fur of an otter, the tail of a beaver, and the bill and feet of a duck. And although the platypus is a mammal, it lays eggs instead of bearing its young alive. Less than one inch long, a platypus's thin-shelled egg is a lot like the egg of a snake or turtle. But the platypus nurses its young with milk—just as cows, dogs, and other mammals do.

The bill of the platypus is covered with skin. It is located at the front of the head—where most other mammals have noses and lips! Its teeth are made of a dense, horny substance. Webs of skin grow between the toes of all four feet. Along with the tail, these webbed feet make the platypus an excellent swimmer and diver.

Because of its reptile-like characteristics, the platypus is assumed to be an ancient animal. Scientists think the platypus descended from a link that existed between reptiles and mammals about 150 million years ago.

At one time, platypuses were killed in large numbers for their fur. For many years, however, platypus-hunting has been forbidden by the Australian government.

COMPREHENSION: Circle a letter.

1. The platypus is in the same "animal family" as
   a. ducks and geese.   b. dogs and cows.

2. The platypus could be described as
   a. strange or weird.
   b. average or routine.

3. Unlike other mammals, the platypus
   a. nurses its young.
   b. lays eggs.

4. The main part of a platypus's diet is
   a. bugs.   b. slugs.

The Platypus   (page 2)

NOTING DETAILS

1. The platypus has the _____ of an otter, the tail of a _____, and the feet of a _____.

2. The teeth of a platypus are made of a dense, horny _____.

3. Because of its _____– _____ characteristics, the platypus is thought to be an ancient animal.

4. Where most other mammals have a nose and lips, the platypus has a _____.

DRAWING CONCLUSIONS

1. On what continent would you find the platypus?
   - _____

2. The phrase "down under" refers to which hemisphere on a globe?
   - _____

3. What island is located just off the southeastern coast of Australia?
   - _____

SYNONYMS OR ANTONYMS? Write S or A.

_____ 1. descended / ascended

_____ 2. sewn / stitched

_____ 3. examined / inspected

_____ 4. enemy / foe

_____ 5. forbidden / allowed

_____ 6. mediocre / excellent

VOCABULARY: Complete the sentences with words from the article.

1. A _____ is a practical joke or a trick to fool others.

2. Scientists who study animals and animal life are called _____.

3. Something that is _____ is not known for certain, but is supposed to be true.

4. _____ are sharp spines, usually found on the legs of birds.

5. A _____ substance is extremely hard and tough.

PICK A PROJECT: Work on the back of this sheet.

- Draw an imaginary animal that is the combination of at least three other animals.

- Name two other mammals that don't look at all like people, apes, horses, etc. Hint: What's the largest animal in the ocean?

It's a Buggy World

Scientists have identified over one million species of animals on Earth. Of these, approximately 800,000 are insects. In fact, there are more insects in one square mile of rural land than there are human beings on the entire Earth! Here are a few more interesting facts about some citizens of our buggy world.

- Just how much do termites eat? A well-established colony 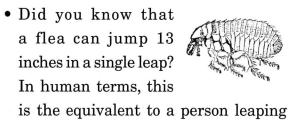 with some 60,000 members will eat only about one-fifth of an ounce of wood a day.

- The hardiest of all the world's insects is the mosquito. This insect is equally comfortable at the North Pole or in an equatorial jungle.

- A housefly can carry germs as far as 15 miles away from the original source of contamination.

- A queen bee can lay up to 1,500 eggs a day. It takes three weeks for these eggs to hatch as mature adults.

- It is estimated that as many as 70 insect species per day become extinct. Today, six species of California butterflies are on the endangered list.

- Did you know that a flea can jump 13 inches in a single leap? In human terms, this  is the equivalent to a person leaping 700 feet in one bound.

- Many insects hear with their hair. By vibrating when they feel sound waves, these hairs send a message to  the insect's central nervous system. The cockroach's sound-receiving hairs are on its abdomen. The hairy caterpillar has "ears" over its entire body.

- There really are such things as cooties. They are a kind of body lice. The word *cootie* comes from the Maylay word *kutu*, meaning "louse."

- Every year, scientists discover from seven to ten thousand new insect species. They suspect there are between one million and 10 million species not yet identified.

It's a Buggy World   (page 2)

COMPREHENSION: Circle a word.

1. Compared to other animals, insects could be described as (dominant / docile).

2. About (80,000 / 800,000) insect species have been identified.

3. One colony of termites (can / can't) eat a large wooden house in a year.

4. The creatures of the insect world are known for their (similarity / variety).

DRAWING CONCLUSIONS: Write **T** for *true* or **F** for *false*.

1. _____ About ⁴/₅ of the world's animals are insects.

2. _____ Houseflies can make people sick.

3. _____ Termites reproduce faster than honeybees.

4. _____ Insects that don't hear with their hair don't hear at all.

LOOK IT UP! Write the dictionary definition.

insect: _____

_____

_____

WORD ANALYSIS

1. The *plural* form of housefly is

_____.

2. The *singular* form of lice is

_____.

VOCABULARY: Complete the sentences with words from the article.

1. A _____ is a group of animals that are alike in some ways.

2. Something described as _____ is on or near the equator.

3. _____ and *threatened* are synonyms.

4. *Partial* and _____ are antonyms.

5. _____ is the act of making something dirty or infectious.

6. A _____ is a group of animals who live together.

7. The words *transport* and _____ are synonyms.

8. The words *urban* and _____ are antonyms.

PICK A PROJECT: Work on the back of this sheet.

● Draw a picture of any insect mentioned in the article.

● Make a crossword puzzle, using any six words from the article.

● Write two new titles for the article.

Annie Oakley

If you've ever seen the musical *Annie Get Your Gun*, you know about Annie Oakley. She joined Buffalo Bill's Wild West Show in 1885 and became a big star throughout the United States and Europe. What did Annie do to gain her fame? She was an expert shot with a pistol, rifle, and shotgun.

Once, with a .22 rifle, Annie accomplished an incredible feat. In a single day, she shot 4,772 glass balls out of 5,000 tossed in the air. At 90 feet, she could hit a playing card with the thin edge toward her. If someone threw a card in the air, she could puncture it five or six times before it fell to the ground! Since then, free tickets with holes punched in them have been called "Annie Oakleys." One daring trick put her name—along with that of the German Crown Prince—in the headlines. At his invitation, she shot a cigarette out of his mouth!

On August 13, 1860, Annie Oakley was born Phoebe Anne Oakley Mozee. Her home was a log cabin in Patterson Township, Ohio. She was only nine when she began shooting. After her father died, she supported her family by shooting small game.

Later, on a visit to Cincinnati, Annie noticed an ad for a "come one, come all" shooting match. She entered, and found herself competing with Frank Butler, a vaudeville star. She won the match and later married Butler, joined his act, and became its star. Only five feet tall, Annie was called "Little Sure Shot."

Annie and her husband toured with Buffalo Bill's Wild West Show for 17 years. Without realizing it, they were helping Buffalo Bill Cody to create a new American industry—the "western hero" business. This industry quickly spread to literature, movies, radio, and rodeos, providing a living for thousands of persons.

COMPREHENSION: Cross out facts that are *not* mentioned or implied in the article.

1. Annie Oakley and Calamity Jane were rival sharpshooters.

2. Annie's eye-hand coordination was excellent.

3. Annie was a celebrity both at home and abroad.

4. Annie eventually married Buffalo Bill.

Annie Oakley (page 2)

NOTING DETAILS

1. What Broadway show was based on the life of Annie Oakley?

   • _____

2. In what state was Annie Oakley born?

   • _____

3. What was Annie Oakley's nickname?

   • _____

4. What three kinds of firearms did Annie use in her act?

   • _____

   • _____

   • _____

DRAWING CONCLUSIONS

1. On her best day, how many glass balls did Annie *fail* to hit? • _____

2. How old was Annie when she joined Buffalo Bill's Wild West Show?   • _____

3. What was Buffalo Bill's last name? • _____

4. In what year did Annie retire from Buffalo Bill's Wild West Show?   • _____

LOOK IT UP! Write the dictionary definition.

vaudeville: _____

_____

_____

CHARACTER STUDY: Circle three words that could describe Annie Oakley.

clumsy   petite   snobbish

confident   unexceptional   gifted

SYNONYMS: Draw a line to make each match.

1. **bold**   a. accomplished

2. **skillful**   b. daring

3. **amazing**   c. expert

4. **achieved**   d. incredible

VOCABULARY: Complete the sentences with words from the article.

1. To _____ something is to make a hole in it with a sharp point.

2. The words *contest* and _____ are synonyms.

3. To create an _____ is to develop a new branch of business.

4. To have _____ is to be well-known and much talked about.

5. The words *sooner* and _____ are antonyms.

6. Word pairs such as *heir* and _____ are called homonyms.

PICK A PROJECT: Work on the back of this sheet.

• Write an ad for a wild west show.

• Describe the difference between a rifle and a shotgun.

Life in the Olden Days: 1960–1970

Young people in the 1960s called themselves the "Now Generation." Many protested adult authority. A popular slogan among college students was "Don't trust anyone over 30." Some young people, called hippies or flower children, created their own culture. They wore long dresses and "love beads," old jeans, and fringed jackets. A good many of the flower children were runaway teenagers.

In November 1963, the unthinkable happened: U.S. President John F. Kennedy was killed by an assassin. And in 1968, President Kennedy's tragic death was followed by the assassinations of his brother Robert and Martin Luther King, Jr. The whole country was stunned. As one reporter wrote, "America has lost its innocence." Another lamentable chapter in the story of the '60s was America's growing involvement in the Vietnam War. (By the time the last American troops left Vietnam in 1973, some 211,500 young Americans had been killed or wounded.)

As always, however, life in America went on—in spite of its problems and disappointments. Rock music soared in popularity. A British group called the Beatles had their first hit. The song was called "I Wanna Hold Your Hand." When the Beatles came to the United States, their concerts broke attendance records. In 1960, 19-year-old Chubby Checker recorded a hot song called "The Twist"—and a new dance craze was born.

In 1963, three out of four Americans lived in a city or suburb. Girls wore long, straight hair, and miniskirts were "in" fashions. Fast food outlets and shopping malls were quickly becoming part of the everyday scene.

Kids were watching more and more television in the 1960s. Howdy Doody, Captain Midnight, and Sky King were favorite TV characters. In 1967, *Star Trek* was first shown on television. The popular series went on for 78 shows. Some parents worried that their children were becoming "couch potatoes." But they got some encouragement in 1969. That year saw the debut of *Sesame Street* and *Mr. Rogers' Neighborhood*—two shows that delivered good educational value.

Life in the Olden Days: 1960–1970   (page 2)

COMPREHENSION: Write **T** for *true* or **F** for *false*.

1. _____ Young people of the '60s wanted to be just like their parents when they reached adulthood.

2. _____ Three great American leaders needlessly lost their lives in the 1960s.

3. _____ Chubby Checker was the star of a rock group called the Beatles.

4. _____ Quality TV programming for children began in the late '60s.

NOTING DETAILS

1. By what other name were "hippies" known?

   • _____

2. Did rural America lose population in the 1960s?

   • _____

3. In the 1960s, what age group of Americans started calling themselves the "Now Generation"?

   • _____

DRAWING CONCLUSIONS: Circle a letter.

1. Many high school and college students of the 1960s could be described as
   a. timid and fearful.
   b. conservative and sedate.
   c. impatient and rebellious.

2. The miniskirts worn in the '60s were
   a. silky and flowing.
   b. short and skimpy.
   c. fringed at the bottom.

VOCABULARY: Complete the sentences with words from the article.

1. Someone with _____ has the power to make decisions and take action.

2. The words *shocked* and _____ are synonyms.

3. A big show put on by a musician or a musical group is called a _____.

4. _____ is the opposite of *guilt*.

5. A very popular *fad* is sometimes called a _____.

LOOK IT UP! Write the dictionary definition.

assassination: _____

_____

_____

PICK A PROJECT: Work on the back of this sheet.

• Write a slogan you think would fit *your* generation.

• Draw a picture of a boy and a girl wearing "hippie" clothes.

Andrew Jackson: A Man of the People

In the election of 1828, Andrew Jackson received twice as many electoral votes as John Quincy Adams. He was the first president born in a log cabin. Earlier presidents had come from well-to-do families. Some, like John Adams, had fine educations. Others, like Thomas Jefferson, were both wealthy landowners *and* well-educated.

Like most Americans, Andrew Jackson came from a poor family. Orphaned at 14, he grew up on the frontier of the Carolinas. Then he moved to Tennessee. By working hard, Jackson became a successful lawyer and landowner. That made him a hero to ordinary Americans. It proved that a poor person could rise to power in the United States. That could never have happened in most other countries.

Jackson had won fame as a general in the War of 1812. He was nicknamed "Old Hickory" because of his toughness. The people in his home state said he was the toughest, bravest, hardest-working man in Tennessee! Yet no matter how high he rose, Jackson always remained a man of the frontier.

Washington had never seen anything like Andrew Jackson's inauguration day. Thousands of people watched him take the oath as the seventh president of the United States. Later, they crowded around him, trying to shake his hand. Most of those congratulating him were rough frontiersmen. Their clothes were made of animal skins, and many chewed big plugs of tobacco. Later, at a party in the White House, the frontiersmen stood on the fancy velvet chairs. Why? They wanted to get a better view of their hero! Lacking in manners, they carelessly spilled food and drink on the beautiful carpet. Some rooms were so crowded that people couldn't get out the door. So the frontiersmen climbed out the windows!

Jackson had a great influence on American political life. Earlier presidents didn't pay much attention to common working people. Jackson, a founder of the Democratic Party, believed that democracy couldn't work without the participation of its ordinary citizens. His slogan was, "Let the people rule." Reelected in 1832, Andrew Jackson became the most popular president since George Washington.

Andrew Jackson: A Man of the People   (page 2)

COMPREHENSION: Write **T** for *true* or **F** for *false*.

1. _____   In 1828, Andrew Jackson won election by a narrow margin.

2. _____   Jackson's friends were different from the usual guests at the White House.

3. _____   Jackson grew up in Tennessee, then moved to the Carolinas.

4. _____   Jackson believed in the wisdom of everyday people.

NOTING DETAILS: Write words from the article to complete the sentences.

1. Andrew Jackson's nickname was

   _____.

2. In the War of 1812, Jackson's military

   rank was _____.

3. Jackson's slogan was _____

   _____.

FACT OR OPINION? Write **F** or **O**.

1. _____   Today's Democratic Party has the same ideals as it did then.

2. _____   The uneducated poor felt they could identify with Andrew Jackson.

DRAWING CONCLUSIONS

1. How many years passed between the War of 1812 and Jackson's election?

   ● _____

2. How do you know that Jackson remained popular through his first term in office?

   ● _____

   _____

VOCABULARY: Complete the sentences with words from the article.

1. Someone who owns property is called

   a _____.

2. The words *motto* and

   _____ are synonyms.

3. _____ votes are cast by representatives of each state.

4. A wilderness region next to a settled

   country is called a _____.

5. The words *parentless* and

   _____ are synonyms.

6. A solemn promise to perform a duty is

   called an _____.

ANTONYMS: Draw a line to make each match.

1. **impoverished**   a. lacking
2. **refined**   b. rough
3. **possessing**   c. rose
4. **plummeted**   d. wealthy

PICK A PROJECT: Work on the back of this sheet.

● Write another good title for the article.

● Create a crossword puzzle, using at least six words from the article. Be sure to write good clues!

Figure Skating: Beauty on Ice

The word *skate* comes from the German word *schake*, meaning "leg bone." In ancient times, that word was a literal description. Why? Because people were attaching polished animal bones to their boots so they could slide on ice. For balance and support, they used sticks to push themselves along. Today, it's hard to believe that slow, clumsy movement turned into one of the world's most graceful sports!

Sports historians think that the first iron blades were attached to wooden soles about 700 years ago. Much later, during the mid-1800s, iron blades were replaced by steel—which stayed sharper longer. Not surprisingly, better skates resulted in better skaters.

Originally, figure skating consisted mostly of rigid, robot-like routines. But an American named Jackson Haines changed all that. A dancer himself, Haines transformed the sport into a stylish version of ballet on ice. In 1864, he toured Europe to popularize his "international style" of skating—and everyone loved it! Figure skating became an Olympic sport in 1908.

Still more changes were ahead. Until 1928, women figure skaters wore long black skating outfits and black boots. Their skating was far from exciting. Then a 15-year-old skater at the Olympics brought figure skating to a different level. This Norwegian teenager's name was Sonja Henie. Her skating style featured dance moves, graceful jumps, and thrilling spins. Both the judges and the audience were amazed. Sonja won the gold medal (the first of three), and women's figure skating was never the same!

In 1943, Dick Button, at age 16, became the youngest United States men's champion ever. In 1948, he became the first American skater to win an Olympic gold medal. Four years later, he won another one. He pioneered a new style of skating that was more athletic and acrobatic. By the end of his skating career, he had won the national title seven times and the world title five times. Today, he is a TV commentator for skating events.

Who holds the all-time record for winning the most U.S. figure skating championships? Even devoted fans of the sport may not have heard of Maribel Vinson. Winning nine national titles between 1928 and 1937, she was surely one of America's greatest figure skaters.

Figure Skating: Beauty on Ice   (page 2)

COMPREHENSION: Circle a word.

1. The first real "blades" for skates were made of (iron / wood).

2. (Dick Button / Jackson Haines) was a dancer betore he was a skater.

3. The (Norwegian / German) word *schake* means "leg bone."

4. Over time, there have been (major / minor) changes in figure skating.

5. Figure skating finally became an (international / Olympic) sport in 1908.

6. A girl from (Norwalk / Norway) brought new excitement to figure skating.

DRAWING CONCLUSIONS

1. Who won more Olympic gold medals— Dick Button or Sonja Henie?

    • _____

2. About how many decades have gone by since Dick Button won his first U.S. championship?

    • _____

3. Before the invention of steel blades, for about how long had iron blades been used?

    • _____

4. Why do you think more skating fans haven't ever heard of Maribel Vinson?

    • _____

ANTONYMS: Write a word from the article next to its *opposite*.

1. *duller* / _____

2. *clumsy* / _____

3. *flexible* / _____

4. *contemporary* / _____

5. *figurative* / _____

VOCABULARY: Complete the sentences with words from the article.

1. The first astronauts _____ travel in outer space.

2. The words *revolutionized* and _____ are synonyms.

3. A _____ offers opinions and explanations about what is happening.

4. The words *countrywide* and _____ have the same meaning.

5. Something that's *new* and *attractive* is often called _____.

6. A *true* and *faithful* fan can be described as _____.

PICK A PROJECT: Work on the back of this sheet.

• Draw a cartoon of a skater using "animal bone" blades.

• Why do you think skating is more popular in northern places than in southern ones? Explain your thinking.

Presidential Trivia

Our nation's chief executives make an interesting study in contrast. The following tidbits of history point out just a few of the fascinating similarities and differences.

- There was no private telephone in the president's own office until Herbert Hoover took over in 1929.

- Only one president—Woodrow Wilson—has held a Ph.D. degree granted by a university.

- At 100 pounds and 5 feet, 4 inches, James Madison was the smallest president.

- All United States presidents have worn eyeglasses.

- Franklin Delano Roosevelt was related to 11 former presidents—six by marriage and five by blood.

- Only one man was elected to the House of Representatives after serving as president: John Quincy Adams.

- In 1841, William Henry Harrison gave the longest inaugural address—nearly two hours. At 8,445 words, the speech was twice as long as any other president's.

- James Buchanan is still the only bachelor to serve as president of the United States.

- Theodore Roosevelt was the first U.S. president to ride in a car *and* to fly in an airplane.

- Before becoming president, Andrew Johnson was taught how to read and write by his wife.

- A special bathtub had to be built for President William Howard Taft, who weighed 350 pounds.

- No president of the United States was an only child.

- Through his paternal grandmother, Harry S. Truman was distantly related to President John Tyler.

- Only one man became Chief Justice of the Supreme Court after serving as president: William Howard Taft.

- Lyndon B. Johnson's presidential address of January 8, 1964 was only 3,059 words in length. But 24 writers had worked on it for six weeks, making 16 major revisions.

- President James Garfield could write Latin with one hand and Greek with the other—simultaneously.

Presidential Trivia (page 2)

COMPREHENSION: Circle a word.

1. (Most / All) U.S. presidents had siblings.

2. James (Madison / Buchanan) was never married.

3. (Andrew Johnson / James Garfield) studied classical languages.

4. Andrew (Jackson / Johnson) was still illiterate when he reached adulthood.

NOTING DETAILS

1. Which president later became a congressman?

   ● _____

2. Which president later became a judge?

   ● _____

3. Which president served most recently?

   ● _____

4. Which president was the first to use modern means of transportation?

   ● _____

5. Which president required a "special order" bathroom fixture?

   ● _____

LOOK IT UP! Write the dictionary definition.

Ph.D.: _____

_____

ANTONYMS: Write a word from the article next to its *opposite*.

1. *closely* /_____

2. *maternal* /_____

3. *differences* /_____

4. *demolished* /_____

VOCABULARY: Complete the sentences with words from the article.

1. Events that happen _____ occur at the same time.

2. The _____ of a document has been partially rewritten.

3. The words *country* and _____ are synonyms.

4. A _____ is a man who has no wife.

5. The words *spectacles* and _____ are synonyms.

6. A _____ is a small piece of interesting information or gossip.

PICK A PROJECT: Work on the back of this sheet.

● Name and describe one family member who is related to you by blood and one who is related by marriage.

● Which president would you most like to have known personally? Explain why.

New Twists on an Old Product

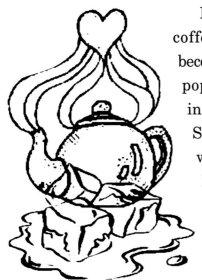

Except for coffee, tea had become the most popular drink in the United States. That's why Richard Blychenden had such high hopes for his trip to St. Louis in 1904. A salesman, Blychenden wanted to promote an Indian tea blend his company exported to America. He'd heard that hundreds of businesses would be showing their wares at the Louisiana Purchase Exhibition. So he'd rented a booth in one of the pavilions and set it up to resemble a teahouse in the Far East. As potential customers passed by, they'd be invited into the booth and offered a cup of freshly brewed hot tea.

But Richard Blychenden was an Englishman. He knew little about the United States and nothing about summertime in St. Louis. The weather was hot and muggy. Visitors to the Exposition didn't want to drink anything hot. Blychenden's teahouse had no customers at all. Had he made a long, expensive trip for nothing? What could the frustrated man do?

No one had ever thought about serving tea any way but hot. But Blychenden decided to serve it cold. First he got a chest full of ice and some tall drinking glasses. Then he filled a glass with ice chips and poured in the hot tea. Next, he made a sign advertising ICED TEA. One passerby tried a glass—then another one did. Soon, a trickle of fairgoers turned into a torrent. *Everyone* wanted to try Blychenden's new copper-colored ice drink. Today, iced tea is America's most popular summertime beverage.

Coincidentally, the tea bag was invented in the same year. Thomas Sullivan, a tea and coffee importer from New York, had no idea he was inventing anything. All he wanted to do was save some money. The tins he'd been using to send out tea samples were becoming increasingly expensive. So he decided to package the tea samples in small, hand-sewn silk bags. His customers were impressed. They thought the silk bags were designed to provide a new brewing technique. Sullivan's business boomed after he accidentally invented the tea bag. The gauze paper tea bag that's used today wasn't invented until 1920.

New Twists on an Old Product (page 2)

COMPREHENSION: Write **T** for *true* or **F** for *false*.

1. _____ The Louisiana Purchase Exposition was held in New York.

2. _____ By 1904, tea was already a favorite drink in America.

3. _____ Thomas Sullivan was a salesman from England.

4. _____ Blychenden cooled the tea before pouring it over ice.

5. _____ A product's packaging can sometimes make the difference between success and failure.

6. _____ A different way to prepare a product might open up a whole new market.

SYNONYMS: Draw a line to make each match.

1. **patrons**   a. wares

2. **humid**   b. muggy

3. **beverage**   c. technique

4. **goods**   d. tins

5. **cans**   e. drink

6. **method**   f. customers

LOOK IT UP! Check a dictionary or encyclopedia for information.

What was the *Louisiana Purchase*?

● _____

_____

DRAWING CONCLUSIONS

For about how many years have people been drinking iced tea?

● _____

VOCABULARY: Complete the sentences with words from the article.

1. A _____ is an open-sided building used for exhibits.

2. An _____ is a large fair or show.

3. A _____ customer is one who hasn't yet bought anything.

4. The words *exporter* and _____ are antonyms.

5. A nonalcoholic drink is _____ when it's steeped in boiled water.

6. Things that are a lot alike are said to _____ each other.

PICK A PROJECT: Work on the back of this sheet.

● What countries produce the most tea? Check an encyclopedia for information.

● Create a crossword puzzle, using at least six words from the article.

● Suggest two alternative titles for the article.

Lunar New Year

People of many Asian cultures celebrate New Year's on the day of the first new moon of the lunar calendar.

TET—Vietnamese New Year

This is a seven-day celebration. Preparations begin weeks in advance. As a fresh start for the year to come, peace and resolution are emphasized.

Traditions

- *Le tru*, a noisy ceremony involving firecrackers, occurs at midnight. Its purpose is to usher out the old and welcome in the new.

- Homes are cleaned and painted.

- Differences between people are resolved and debts are paid.

Special Items

- Families plant a tree called *cay neu* (which can be symbolized by a bamboo pole) in front of their homes. For good luck, it is wrapped in red paper.

- Fortunes are told by using *xam the*, a bamboo jar filled with numbered wooden sticks. The corresponding fortune is read by a *kim loc*, a fortune teller.

SUN NEEN—Chinese New Year

This celebration also marks the beginning of spring. To ensure a prosperous new year, special attention is paid to food, flowers, and unfinished business.

Traditions

- Firecrackers and the lion dance ward off evil spirits.

- Families gather and pay respect to their ancestors.

- Debts are paid and differences resolved.

- *Lei see* (red envelopes filled with money) are given for luck.

Special Items

- Flowers (plum, quince, water lilies, peach blossoms) represent prosperity.

- Candy on a round tray represents sweetness and togetherness.

- Tangerines and oranges, representing long life, are served.

- A whole fish represents prosperity.

SOL—Korean New Year

Korean New Year is focused on good fortune in the family. Often, both January 1 and the Lunar New Year are celebrated.

Traditions

- In a ritual called *Jishin Balpgi*, loud gongs and drums scare away the evil spirits of the old year.

- Respect is shown to ancestors and elders by bowing and kneeling.

Special Items

- Children receive lucky money after honoring their elders with a New Year's bow called *sae-bae*.

- Families eat a breakfast of rice-cake soup.

- Traditional clothing called *hanbok* is worn.

Lunar New Year (page 2)

COMPREHENSION: Circle a word.

1. (Prosperity / Peace) and resolution are the main themes of *Tet*.

2. Families clean and paint their homes to celebrate (Korean / Vietnamese) New Year.

3. To the (Koreans / Chinese), a whole fish stands for wealth.

NOTING DETAILS

1. What do you call a Vietnamese fortune teller?
   * _____

2. What instruments are played at *Jishin Balpgi*?
   * _____

3. How long does it take a family to get ready for Tet?
   * _____

4. Which two cultures celebrate New Year by settling conflicts and paying debts?
   * _____

5. The children of which culture receive "lucky money"?
   * _____

6. Gifts of red envelopes filled with money are presented by people from which country?
   * _____

VOCABULARY: Complete the sentences with words from the article.

1. A _____ crater could only be found on the moon.

2. The words *customs* and _____ are synonyms.

3. The woody stems of _____ are hollow and jointed.

4. On Valentine's Day, love is often _____ by a heart.

5. A _____ is an act performed according to strict rules and in a serious way.

6. The words *honor* and _____ are synonyms.

ANTONYMS: Draw a line to make each match.

1. **impoverished**   a. unfinished
2. **completed**   b. prosperous
3. **offspring**   c. midnight
4. **noon**   d. ancestors

PICK A PROJECT: Work on the back of this sheet.

* Draw a picture of *lei see*.

* Tell about one of your family's New Year's traditions.

* Suggest two alternative titles for the article.

ANSWER KEY

THE AMAZING CHARLIE PARKHURST, page 1

COMPREHENSION

1. c   2. b   3. c   4. b

WHY OR WHY NOT?

Possible answers:

1. No. Women of that time were not allowed to seek adventure.
2. No. He had a scarred face and only one eye.

SYNONYMS

1. e   2. a   3. f   4. b   5. d   6. c

ANTONYMS

1. man   2. tame   3. dressed   4. unusual
5. enjoying   6. attractive

DRAWING CONCLUSIONS

1. 67   2. the horses

ARE YOU AFRAID OF DOGS? page 3

COMPREHENSION

1. b   2. a   3. b   4. b

AUTHOR'S PURPOSE

Probable answer: To inform. A goal of the Humane Society is to educate the public about animals.

NOTING DETAILS

1. to defend its master, its home, and itself
2. to chase and catch anything running away

FIGURATIVE LANGUAGE

c

VOCABULARY

1. a   2. b   3. c   4. b   5. b

HAVE YOU EVER HAD HIC-HICCUPS? page 5

COMPREHENSION

1. T   2. F   3. F   4. T

VOCABULARY

1. breathing   2. Slaughtering   3. rhythm
4. married   5. halts   6. normal   7. contracts

FACT OR OPINION?

1. O   2. O   3. F   4. F

NOTING DETAILS

1. He married twice and fathered eight children.
2. He was getting ready to slaughter a hog; he was a hog farmer.

WORD ANALYSIS

"full of"; Answers will vary.

WARRIOR BEES, page 7

COMPREHENSION

2, 4, 5, 1, 3

RECALLING DETAILS

1. Turkey   2. rhododendron, azalea
3. Pompey the Great

LOOK IT UP!

1. a   2. c   3. a

VOCABULARY

1. Pollen   2. catapult   3. incorporated   4. defensive   5. seize   6. poison   7. distracted

DRAWING CONCLUSIONS

1. b   2. c

THE ENGLISH LANGUAGE: FACTS AND FIGURES, page 9

COMPREHENSION

1. T   2. F   3. F   4. T   5. F   6. T   7. T   8. F

VOCABULARY

1. average   2. countries/territories   3. non-native
4. approximate   5. interesting   6. original

WORDS IN CONTEXT

1. international   2. languages
3. Anglo-Saxon and Latin

LOOK IT UP!

Approximate answers:

fluent: having facility in language use; flowing effortlessly/smoothly

exclusive: not shared with others; independent or single; complete; whole

LIFE IN THE OLDEN DAYS: 1910–1920, page 11

COMPREHENSION

1. F   2. T   3. F   4. F   5. F   6. F

DRAWING CONCLUSIONS

Possible answers:

1. on a clothesline in the sun
2. Water had to be brought in from an outdoor well.
3. cross out: laundromat, power drill, computer

SYNONYMS

1. c   2. a   3. b

NOTING DETAILS

1. wheels   2. sled   3. gas, kerosene

VOCABULARY

1. patent   2. romantic   3. route

PLEASE EXPLAIN

Possible answer: because radio was an exciting new technology; they wanted to experiment.

THE HISTORY OF GYMNASTICS, page 13

COMPREHENSION

1. b 2. b 3. a

NOTING DETAILS

1. ignored 2. Roman 3. physical

BEFORE OR AFTER?

1. after 2. after 3. before

ANTONYMS

1. d 2. a 3. b 4. c

VOCABULARY

1. event 2. emperor 3. competition
4. disappeared 5. trained 6. discus, javelin
7. Tumbling 8. comeback

THE MOST SOCIABLE MAMMAL, page 15

COMPREHENSION

1. F 2. T 3. F 4. T 5. T 6. T

DRAWING CONCLUSIONS

Probable answers:
1. Rain might flood and ruin the prairie dog's home.
2. They live together in a community.

ANTONYMS

1. d 2. c 3. b 4. a

SYNONYMS

1. b 2. d 3. a 4. c

NOTING DETAILS

1. the western part of North America from Canada in the north to Mexico in the south
2. coyotes, rattlesnakes, burrowing owls

VOCABULARY

1. young 2. shrill 3. mammal
4. Beady 5. Alfalfa 6. tunnel

MONEY IN HISTORY, page 17

COMPREHENSION

1. T 2. F 3. F 4. F 5. T

NOTING DETAILS

1. "Mind Your Own Business" 2. the obol 3. 4
4. in Greece; to keep the tiny coins from getting lost

DRAWING CONCLUSIONS

1. b 2. a

VOCABULARY

1. feather 2. cash 3. skull 4. clam

WONDERFUL STEVIE, page 19

COMPREHENSION

cross out: 1 and 4

NOTING DETAILS

1. Detroit, Michigan 2. rhythm and blues
3. Braille 4. blind 5. harmonica, drums, piano, organ

CHARACTER STUDY

circle: innovative, gifted, admired

ANTONYMS

1. Poor 2. hired

DRAWING CONCLUSIONS

1. b 2. a 3. a

SYNONYMS

1. b 2. d 3. a 4. c

THE LITTLE RASCALS, page 21

COMPREHENSION

1. F 2. F 3. T 4. F

NOTING DETAILS

1. Darla 2. dollhouse, playhouse, clubhouse
3. mudpies 4. Stymie

ANTONYMS

1. b 2. d 3. a 4. c

VOCABULARY

1. b 2. c 3. c

BEFORE OR AFTER?

1. after 2. after

PLEASE EXPLAIN

Movies were made over a 22-year period; the original actors would have become adults.

THE BAD OLD DAYS OF BASKETBALL, page 23

COMPREHENSION

1. T 2. T 3. T 4. F

NOTING DETAILS

1. stoves, radiators
2. padded pants, knee guards, elbow pads
3. hatpins, nails
4. Pennsylvania

SYNONYMS

1. b 2. d 3. e 4. c 5. a

VOCABULARY

1. gymnasium 2. court 3. fans 4. Referees

ANTONYMS

1. extraordinary 2. chilled 3. mournful 4. pulled

KRAKATOA ERUPTS, page 25

COMPREHENSION

1. T 2. F 3. F 4. T

NOTING DETAILS

1. spider 2. island 3. two 4. rock, ash

DRAWING CONCLUSIONS

1. 120 2. one-fourth 3. 3 4. 1,000 5. 20

PLEASE EXPLAIN

No people lived on Krakatoa.

VOCABULARY

1. exploded 2. settlements 3. synonyms
4. catastrophe 5. speck 6. trembled

SOME SUNNY FACTS, page 27

COMPREHENSION

1. its center 2. rotates and moves ahead

WORDS IN CONTEXT

1. volume 2. radiation

NOTING DETAILS

1. 43,000 miles per hour 2. Betelgeuse
3. their inner nuclei are exposed

LOOK IT UP!

1. nucleus 2. having to do with the sun

DRAWING CONCLUSIONS

1. $5\frac{1}{2}$ 2. less 3. .2 4. Centigrade

SYNONYMS

1. b 2. c 3. d 4. a

ANTONYMS

1. exposing 2. bright 3. completing

WHY IS ENGLISH HARD TO LEARN? page 29

COMPREHENSION

1. are not 2. are not 3. can

COMPREHENSION

1. F 2. F 3. T

VOCABULARY

1. does 2. refuse 3. sow 4. present
5. desert 6. wound 7. intimate 8. produce

INFERENCE

1. b 2. c

COMPOUND WORDS

1. farmland 2. birthday 3. overfilled

LOOK IT UP!

1. a sick or disabled person 2. to force to undergo

WHATEVER HAPPENED TO THE PASSENGER PIGEON?, page 31

COMPREHENSION

1. 20th 2. eastern 3. food

NOTING DETAILS

1. 1914 2. southwest 3. Chicago and New York
4. Kentucky and Ohio

LOOK IT UP!

rapid motion back and forth

COMPREHENSION

1. synonyms 2. 12 months 3. faint 4. unusual
5. approximate 6. flock 7. birds

COMPARING PREHISTORIC ANIMALS, page 33

COMPREHENSION

1. F 2. T 3. T 4. F 5. T 6. F 7. T

DRAWING CONCLUSIONS

1. a 2. c 3. b

SYNONYMS

1. d 2. c 3. a 4. b

LOOK IT UP!

country in east central Asia

NOTING DETAILS

1. king crab 2. tuatara

MAILMEN ON HORSEBACK, page 35

COMPREHENSION

1. T 2. F 3. T 4. F

NOTING DETAILS

1. Overland Mail 2. steamship

DRAWING CONCLUSIONS

1. $1\frac{1}{2}$ years 2. 2,000 3. 5 4. telegraph

VOCABULARY

1. c 2. a 3. b 4. a

HOMONYMS

1. mail 2. weather 3. rode 4. night

HOW WELL DO YOU KNOW YOUR BODY? page 37

COMPREHENSION

1. N 2. Y 3. Y 4. Y 5. N 6. Y

NOTING DETAILS

1. sticky mucus
2. to carry blood to every part of the body
3. nerve signals
4. the skin
5. about 60

INFERENCE

80% of all body heat escapes through the head

LOOK IT UP!

the clear outer layer of the eyeball

VOCABULARY

1. Cells 2. corrosive 3. Mucus 4. reconstitute

PRODUCE: IS IT RIPE? IS IT READY? page 39

COMPREHENSION

1. F 2. T 3. F 4. F 5. T 6. T

NOTING DETAILS

1. Raspberries 2. cantaloupe, watermelon
3. a husk, silk 4. green

LOOK IT UP!

shell that holds a plant's seeds

VOCABULARY

1. c 2. b 3. a 4. b 5. a 6. c

LIFE IN THE OLDEN DAYS: 1920–1930, page 41

COMPREHENSION

1. a 2. c

SYNONYMS

1. c 2. d 3. a 4. b

ANTONYMS

1. abrupt 2. newcomer 3. sundown

NOTING DETAILS

1. Grand Ole Opry 2. dance
3. country music group 4. penicillin 5. children

VOCABULARY

1. Tenements 2. amendment 3. jukebox

A PRESIDENT'S FIRST SPEECH, page 43

COMPREHENSION

1. beginning 2. Constitution
3. Lincoln 4. 1933 5. oath

NOTING DETAILS

1. 4 2. March 4 3. no
4. America's Civil War between North and South

SYNONYMS

1. preserve, protect, defend 2. address
3. malice

VOCABULARY

1. cherish 2. oath 3. goals 4. unity

DRAWING CONCLUSIONS

cold; sometimes snowy

ANCIENT INVENTIONS, page 45

COMPREHENSION

1. F 2. T 3. T 4. F 5. F

NOTING DETAILS

1. stone 2. plow 3. Greek

DRAWING CONCLUSIONS

silk

LOOK IT UP!

fine, white, hard earthenware used in making
bathtubs, sinks, dishes, vases, etc.

VOCABULARY

1. motive 2. plow 3. lathe 4. Papyrus

ANTONYMS

1. c 2. d 3. a 4. b

BEFORE OR AFTER?

1. before 2. after 3. before

RULES OF THUMB, page 47

COMPREHENSION

1. c 2. b 3. c

DRAWING CONCLUSIONS

1. P 2. RT 3. P 4. RT

LOOK IT UP!

8 ft. long, 4 ft. wide, 4 ft. high

SYNONYMS OR ANTONYMS?

1. S 2. S 3. A 4. A 5. S

VOCABULARY

1. heifers 2. diameter 3. radius
4. a shot in the dark

LIFE IN THE OLDEN DAYS: 1930–1940, page 49

COMPREHENSION

1. b 2. b 3. a 4. c 5. b

DRAWING CONCLUSIONS

Dust Bowl

FACT OR OPINION?

1. O 2. F 3. F

VOCABULARY

1. evicted 2. drought 3. denounced

WHAT'S A GEYSER? page 51

COMPREHENSION

1. F 2. F 3. T 4. T 5. F 6. F

NOTING DETAILS

1. the Giantess 2. 175 feet
3. It seeps back into the ground. 4. 200

LOOK IT UP!

northwestern Wyoming

SYNONYMS

1. d 2. a 3. b 4. c

VOCABULARY

1. solution 2. spring 3. Intervals
4. Minerals 5. Steam

THE HISTORY OF GLIDERS, page 53

COMPREHENSION

1. an engine 2. soar 3. 20th 4. England

NOTING DETAILS

1. light tanks 2. 900 feet
3. shoulders and feet 4. 101 years

LOOK IT UP!

hinged wing flaps that can be moved up or
down to steady a plane

YOUR OPINION, PLEASE

Possible answer: No; because he made his
coachman take experimental glider flights

VOCABULARY

1. rudder 2. revived 3. Artillery
4. transporting 5. enthusiasts

CLOUDS, CLOUDS, AND MORE CLOUDS! page 55

COMPREHENSION

1. c 2. b 3. a

DRAWING CONCLUSIONS

1. low 2. higher

NOTING DETAILS

1. stratus 2. cirrus 3. cirro-stratus, cirro-cumulus

ANTONYMS

1. heights 2. shapeless 3. summer
4. dull 5. early 6. often

SYNONYMS

1. heaps 2. main 3. ringlet 4. classified 5. still

PROVERBS: WISDOM IN A NUTSHELL, page 57

COMPREHENSION

1. T 2. F 3. T 4. T 5. T

MATCHING MEANINGS

1. 3 2. 2 3. 10

SYNONYMS

1. b 2. d 3. a 4. c

ANTONYMS

1. secretly, publicly 2. winter, summer

VOCABULARY

1. Wisdom 2. Practical 3. Flattery
4. correct 5. loom

THE TERRIFYING TOMATO, page 59

COMPREHENSION

cross out: 1 and 4

NOTING DETAILS

1. Spain 2. Thomas Jefferson 3. nightshade
4. Dr. Miles's Compound Extract of Tomato
5. A and C

DRAWING CONCLUSIONS

1. 1865 2. 500 3. 18th and 19th

SYNONYMS

1. popular 2. poisonous 3. terrifying 4. rumor

ANTONYMS

1. c 2. e 3. d 4. b 5. a

VOCABULARY

1. greenhouse 2. source 3. colonists
4. courthouse

LOOK IT UP!

ketchup

A STORY BEHIND EVERY WORD, page 61

COMPREHENSION

1. F 2. T 3. T 4. T

NOTING DETAILS

1. hamstrung 2. sniper 3. mascot
4. sniper and bigwig

WORD ANALYSIS

1. blockbuster, hamstrung, bigwig 2. hamstrung

VOCABULARY

1. wary 2. judge 3. medieval
4. fate 5. deliberately 6. Etymology

LOOK IT UP!

anything that shows how genuine
or pure something is

TWO UNUSUAL PIRATES, page 63

COMPREHENSION

1. c 2. b 3. b 4. c

LOOK IT UP!

east

DRAWING CONCLUSIONS

1. skull and crossbones 2. Jamaica

SYNONYMS

1. haunts 2. captives 3. plunder
4. hangman

VOCABULARY

1. seldom 2. daredevil 3. cutlass
4. sloop 5. postponed 6. pirate

LIFE IN THE OLDEN DAYS: 1940–1950, page 65

COMPREHENSION

1. c 2. a 3. b 4. c

COMPARING PAST AND PRESENT

Answers will vary.

VOCABULARY

1. allowed 2. dominated 3. vacant 4. skinny
5. fashions 6. stump 7. designated 8. drills

THE LAST OF ITS KIND, page 67

COMPREHENSION

1. T 2. F 3. T 4. F 5. F 6. T

NOTING DETAILS

1. Crocodiles 2. cold 3. largest 4. head

DRAWING CONCLUSIONS

circle: unique, coldblooded, scaly

LOOK IT UP!

a preliminary explanation about how or why something happens

SYNONYMS

1. e 2. b 3. c 4. a 5. d 6. g 7. f

ANTONYMS

1. gradually 2. threatened 3. active 4. early

DEVOTED DADDIES, page 69

COMPREHENSION

1. marmoset, arrow poison frog, rhea 2. rhea
3. The rhea, arrow poison frog, and marmoset live in South America. 4. arrow poison frog
5. rhea 6. jacana 7. arrow poison frog

NOTING DETAILS

1. toes 2. turkeys 3. jungle 4. jacana

VOCABULARY

1. nurturing 2. devoted 3. incubate 4. compost
5. relinquishes 6. deposits

ANTONYMS

1. aggressive 2. drab 3. female
4. briefly 5. primary

EVER SEEN A FALLING STAR?, page 71

COMPREHENSION

1. F 2. T 3. F 4. F 5. T

NOTING DETAILS

1. enter 2. seconds 3. explodes 4. Meteors

LOOK IT UP!

science dealing with the atmosphere, especially weather conditions

DRAWING CONCLUSIONS

1. They circle around the sun.
2. nearly 100 years ago

SYNONYMS

1. scorched 2. bright 3. observe 4. velocity

VOCABULARY

1. obliterate 2. vaporized
3. unobstructed 4. matter

DRAWING CONCLUSIONS

circle: swift, bright, solid

WORLD HERITAGE SITES , page 73

COMPREHENSION

1. Kentucky 2. Washington 3. Seminole
4. two 5. older 6. Alaska

NOTING DETAILS

1. Lechuguilla Cave 2. Colorado River
3. the Sierra Nevadas 4. Pacific

DRAWING CONCLUSIONS

1. about 3,400 years ago 2. Grand Canyon

VOCABULARY

1. Stalactites, stalagmites 2. glacier 3. monolith
4. adaptation 5. network 6. temperate

LIFE IN THE OLDEN DAYS: 1950–1960, page 75

COMPREHENSION

1. television 2. 17 3. Boys 4. rock 'n' roll

NOTING DETAILS

1. Davy, Kangaroo, Doody 2. Disneyland

FACT OR OPINION?

1. O 2. O 3. F

VOCABULARY

1. junk foods 2. Suburbs 3. debut 4. Coonskin
5. generation 6. survey 7. lunchboxes

THE WORLD'S OLDEST STORIES, page 77

COMPREHENSION

1. F 2. T 3. T 4. F 5. F 6. T

LOOK IT UP!

legend: old story handed down through the years, usually meant to explain how something came to be
myth: stories made up by ancient peoples to explain the world around them

DRAWING CONCLUSIONS

Myths are not based on real events.

ANTONYMS

1. enormous 2. answer 3. natural
4. morning 5. wonderful 6. forgotten

VOCABULARY

1. scholars 2. nymph 3. Virtues
4. aesthetics 5. chariot 6. murmuring

SYNONYMS

1. d 2. c 3. a 4. b

THE OLDEST LIVING THINGS, page 79

COMPREHENSION

1. Redwoods, sequoias 2. thousands 3. enemies 4. more 5. circumference 6. slowly

DRAWING CONCLUSIONS

1. 4 2. It cracks too easily to be useful.
3. No. They are evergreens.

NOTING DETAILS

1. They are not subject to disease or insect attack.
2. the Sierra Nevada Mountains in California
3. lightning

VOCABULARY

1. Groves 2. disease 3. Fragments
4. acre 5. timber

ANTONYMS

1. a 2. d 3. b 4. c

BASEBALL: THE CHANGING GAME , page 81

COMPREHENSION

cross out: 1 and 3

NOTING DETAILS

1. Houston 2. It rolls faster and bounces higher.
3. base-ball 4. Elysian Fields

DRAWING CONCLUSIONS

1. harder 2. There were no set fielding positions.
3. about 100 years

SYNONYMS

1. b 2. d 3. a 4. c

LOOK IT UP!

In Greek myths, the place where good people go when they die.

VOCABULARY

1. skyrocket 2. Contracts 3. major

THE PLATYPUS, page 83

COMPREHENSION

1. b 2. a 3. b 4. a

NOTING DETAILS

1. fur, beaver, duck 2. substance
3. reptile-like 4. bill

DRAWING CONCLUSIONS

1. Australia 2. southern 3. Tasmania

SYNONYMS OR ANTONYMS?

1. A 2. S 3. S 4. S 5. A 6. A

VOCABULARY

1. hoax 2. zoologists 3. assumed
4. Spurs 5. horny

IT'S A BUGGY WORLD, page 85

COMPREHENSION

1. dominant 2. 800,000 3. can't 4. variety

DRAWING CONCLUSIONS

1. T 2. T 3. F 4. F

LOOK IT UP!

small animal with six legs, usually two pairs of wings, and a head, thorax, and abdomen

WORD ANALYSIS

1. houseflies 2. louse

VOCABULARY

1. species 2. equatorial 3. Endangered
4. entire 5. Contamination 6. colony
7. carry 8. rural

ANNIE OAKLEY, page 87

COMPREHENSION

cross out: 1 and 4

NOTING DETAILS

1. Annie Get Your Gun 2. Ohio
3. Little Sure Shot 4. pistol, rifle, shotgun

DRAWING CONCLUSIONS

1. 228 2. 25 3. Cody 4. 1902

LOOK IT UP!

stage show comprised of different kinds of acts, such as skits, songs, dances, etc.

CHARACTER STUDY

circle: petite, confident, gifted

SYNONYMS

1. b 2. c 3. d 4. a

VOCABULARY

1. puncture 2. match 3. industry
4. fame 5. later 6. air

LIFE IN THE OLDEN DAYS: 1960–1970, page 89

COMPREHENSION

1. F 2. T 3. F 4. T

NOTING DETAILS

1. flower children 2. yes 3. young people

DRAWING CONCLUSIONS

1. c 2. b

VOCABULARY

1. authority 2. stunned 3. concert
4. Innocence 5. craze

LOOK IT UP!

the act of murdering a government leader or other important person, usually for political reasons

ANDREW JACKSON: A MAN OF THE PEOPLE, page 91

COMPREHENSION

1. F 2. T 3. F 4. T

NOTING DETAILS

1. Old Hickory 2. general 3. Let the people rule.

FACT OR OPINION?

1. O 2. F

DRAWING CONCLUSIONS

1. 16 years 2. He was reelected for a second term.

VOCABULARY

1. landowner 2. slogan 3. Electoral 4. frontier
5. orphaned 6. oath

ANTONYMS

1. d 2. b 3. a 4. c

FIGURE SKATING: BEAUTY ON ICE, page 93

COMPREHENSION

1. iron 2. Jackson Haines 3. German
4. major 5. Olympic 6. Norway

DRAWING CONCLUSIONS

1. Sonja Henie 2. about 6 decades
3. about 500 years
4. because she skated so long ago

ANTONYMS

1. sharper 2. graceful 3. rigid
4. ancient 5. literal

VOCABULARY

1. pioneered 2. transformed 3. commentator
4. national 5. stylish 6. devoted

PRESIDENTIAL TRIVIA, page 95

COMPREHENSION

1. All 2. Buchanan 3. James Garfield
4. Johnson

NOTING DETAILS

1. John Quincy Adams 2. William Howard Taft
3. Lyndon B. Johnson 4. Theodore Roosevelt
5. William Howard Taft

LOOK IT UP!

Doctor of Philosophy

ANTONYMS

1. distantly 2. paternal 3. similarities 4. built

VOCABULARY

1. simultaneously 2. revision 3. nation
4. bachelor 5. eyeglasses 6. tidbit

NEW TWISTS ON AN OLD PRODUCT, page 97

COMPREHENSION

1. F 2. T 3. F 4. F 5. T 6. T

SYNONYMS

1. f 2. b 3. e 4. a 5. d 6. c

LOOK IT UP!

land bought by the U.S. from France in 1803 for $15 million

DRAWING CONCLUSIONS

about 100 years

VOCABULARY

1. pavilion 2. exposition 3. potential
4. importer 5. brewed 6. resemble

LUNAR NEW YEAR, page 99

COMPREHENSION

1. Peace 2. Vietnamese 3. Chinese

NOTING DETAILS

1. kim loc 2. gongs and drums 3. weeks
4. Chinese and Vietnamese 5. Korean
6. China

VOCABULARY

1. lunar 2. traditions 3. bamboo
4. symbolized 5. ceremony 6. respect

ANTONYMS

1. b 2. a 3. d 4. c